# Human Resource Management in the Knowledge Economy

## New Challenges • New Roles • New Capabilities

Mark L. Lengnick-Hall
Cynthia A. Lengnick-Hall

16pt

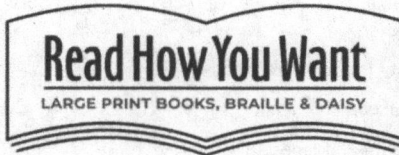

# Copyright Page from the Original Book

## Human Resource Management in the Knowledge Economy

Berrett-Koehler Publishers, Inc.
235 Montgomery Street, Suite 650
San Francisco, California 94104-2916
Tel: (415) 288-0260, Fax: (415) 362-2512
www.bkconnection.com

Ordering information for print editions
*Quantity sales.* Special discounts are available on quantity purchases by corporations,
associations, and others. For details, contact the "Special Sales Department" at the
Berrett-Koehler address above.
*Individual sales.* Berrett-Koehler publications are available through most bookstores.
They can also be ordered directly from Berrett-Koehler: Tel: (800) 929-2929; Fax:
(802) 864-7626; www.bkconnection.com
*Orders for college textbook/course adoption use.* Please contact Berrett-Koehler:
Tel: (800) 929-2929; Fax: (802) 864-7626.
*Orders by U.S. trade bookstores and wholesalers.* Please contact Ingram Publisher
Services, Tel: (800) 509-4887; Fax: (800) 838-1149; E-mail: customer
.service@ingrampublisherservices.com; or visit www.ingrampublisherservices.com/
Ordering for details about electronic ordering.

Berrett-Koehler and the BK logo are registered trademarks of Berrett-Koehler
Publishers, Inc.

First Edition
Paperback print edition ISBN 978-1-57675-159-6
PDF e-book ISBN 978-1-60994-183-3
IDPF e-book ISBN 978-1-60994-599-2

2011-1

Publication Services, design

Greg Whitlock, copyeditor

Jessica Matthews, indexer;

Philip Hamer and Jenny Putman, proofreaders

Paul R. Mitchell, production coordinator

Steven M. Sansone, setup and typesetting

# TABLE OF CONTENTS

# Tables

*To our daughters,*
*Rebecca and Amanda,*
*who are getting ready*
*to enter the knowledge economy*

# Preface

"We have met the enemy, and he is us."
—Pogo

The human resource management function in organizations is in need of a reexamination to determine whether simply doing what it has always done—only perhaps better—will meet the challenges of the emerging, knowledge-based economy. We think the answer to this question is a definite "NO!" In the same way that the United States military has developed exceptional technological prowess—yet has found that the conventional military approach is inadequate for fighting terrorists—the human resource management function that evolved to address the needs of the industrial era is insufficient to meet the needs of the knowledge era.

In our many years of teaching, researching, and consulting in the area of human resource management (HRM), we have observed a number of significant trends. First, the human resource (HR) arena in many firms is seen as a set of discrete functions, or subsystems, each finely honed to meet a particular need or accomplish a particular set of tasks. Staffing subsystems, when done well, put the right person in the right place at the right time. Compensation systems motivate performance and encourage employee retention.

Other systems are designed to perform equally focused tasks.

Second, by the end of the twentieth century, many organizations had developed well-integrated HRM systems, with each of the subsystems working together harmoniously to enhance the firm's overall human performance. For example, staffing, compensation, and training subsystems can provide synergistic support for each other and thereby enhance a firm's ability to achieve its strategic objectives. Often, particular HRM techniques were selected to augment a specific strategy or source of competitive advantage, such as low cost or innovation.

Third, by the end of the twentieth century, many organizations had begun to outsource some of these HRM subsystems. The assumption was that external specialists could provide greater efficiency and effectiveness, at least in the short term. The long-term results of disaggregating the HRM system of an organization and delegating some of these activities to outside vendors are, at present, unclear. However, we suspect that one unintended cost is the erosion of a firm's expertise for managing the full range of its human capital.

Fourth, technology, and in particular, information technology, has made it possible for organizations to deliver HRM service to both managers and employees that is better than in the past if one uses conventional measures to assess HRM activities. Furthermore, in most organizations, technology has made it possible to reduce the size of the HRM staff without reducing services.

Fifth, human capital has moved from a secondary, supportive role to a primary, central role in helping organizations achieve a competitive advantage. Increasingly, firms have come to realize that people are a primary source of rare, inimitable, flexible capabilities. Unfortunately, HRM staff members are not always seen as equally crucial in capitalizing on this competitive resource.

Together, all five of these trends have resulted in what might be described as a "leaner, meaner HRM function." HRM still does many of the same things it did when industrial organizations came into being at the turn of the twentieth century—however, today these activities are done more efficiently and effectively, with fewer people and more technology.

If the economic environment were to continue to develop along the same trajectory that it has in the past, the HR practices that had evolved by the end of the twentieth century would be adequate to meet the needs of organizations in the twenty-first century. Remember, dinosaurs had evolved into complex organisms that mastered the environment they confronted—had that environment not changed, they would still be around! However, just as changes in the dinosaurs' environment no longer favored their physical adaptations—and ultimately led to their extinction—changes in the economic conditions facing organizations in the twenty-first century could likewise lead to the extinction, or at least downgrading, of the importance and form of the HRM department in many business firms.

Human resource management policies, programs, and practices that served companies well in the industrial era (such as job descriptions or traditional overtime policies) will not be adequate for the challenges of the new, knowledge-based economy. A number of less familiar characteristics shape the competitive landscape in the emerging business setting. The context for decision-making and action has changed as jobs and roles are continuously redefined. This is coupled with external conflicts of interest as industry boundaries blur and customers are given a wider range of choices. Organizations must operate effectively in the face of uncertainty caused by incomplete, inaccurate, and contradictory information. The stream of unfamiliar and unanalyzed data and observations that organizations receive is relentless. The market landscape is extremely fluid. Each episode a firm experiences is the temporary result of a unique combination of circumstances, often requiring a unique solution. Events are shaped by the specific incidents that precede them, the particular interpretation enacted by decision makers at the moment, and the specific mission of the firm wanting to take action.

Learning organizations not only develop new understandings, they also have the ability to alter their behavior to conform to what they learn. Continuous change requires improvisation and often mandates a departure from initial plans. It is essential for firms to recognize that people, rather than technologies or process, are best able to sense and make judgments that put structure around the inevitable disorder that results from these forces. Therefore, the knowledge economy, more than any previous market trend, places a premium on human talents. Consequently, the management of a firm's HR, more broadly defined than ever before, will be pivotal in determining the ultimate success or failure of the organization.

For companies to compete effectively in this new environment, they must be flexible, adaptable, and adjustable. Companies must manage their intellectual capital as deliberately and effectively as they do their tangible assets. To do this, HRM must assume new roles to meet these new challenges.

As more organizations have recognized the importance of human capital and knowledge management with respect to competitive success, it is reasonable to expect that HR professionals would be at the forefront of organizational leadership. Yet, to the contrary, the importance of activities performed by HRM units seems to be losing ground in a majority of organizations, while other functional areas (for example, information technology, operations, finance) gain greater and greater influence. In most cases, HRM appears to be playing a secondary role at a time when the ability to harness a firm's human capital should be more in demand and more valued than ever before. Why is this occurring? Why are so many firms content to trust external vendors to do the conventional work of HRM professionals?

Human resource management continues to be criticized for its operational and bureaucratic focus and its inability to keep up with changes in the environment. While the forces of the market have radically altered the workplace, HR policies, programs, and practices have been slow to adapt and have even more rarely taken the lead in helping firms capitalize on unprecedented opportunities. Human resource management has typically focused its attention on honing its ability to do the same kinds of things better and better rather than to consider an entirely different kind of contribution.

This book provides a blueprint for change for HRM activities and contributions in the knowledge economy. It identifies the most important features of the knowledge economy and details four primary roles that HRM professionals must adopt to meet these new challenges effectively. A secondary purpose of this book is to stimulate HRM professionals to think beyond a simple operational focus on attracting, selecting, developing, retaining, and utilizing employees to a more strategic focus on managing human capital and managing knowledge.

It is our hope that this book will provide the stimulus for change.

Special thanks to the people at Publication Services who helped make this book a reality: Paul Mitchell coordinated the production of the project, Gregory Whitlock copyedited and reviewed each word of the manuscript, and Susie Yates, customer service representative, kept all of us on the same page.

We would like to express our deepest appreciation to Steven Piersanti and Jeevan Sivasubramaniam of Berrett-Koehler for their continued support and unwavering understanding throughout this project. Their concern and responsiveness helped us enormously throughout a very challenging period.

Mark L. Lengnick-Hall
Cynthia A. Lengnick-Hall


San Antonio, Texas
September 2002

# Chapter 1

# A New Imperative for Human Resource Management

"The secret of business is to know something that nobody else knows."
—Aristotle Onassis

"In a time of drastic change it is the learners who inherit the future. The learned usually find themselves equipped to live in a world that no longer exists."
—Eric Hoffer

Pick up almost any business book or magazine and one is sure to see claims that a firm's people are its most important resource. Unfortunately for most organizations, the ability to capitalize on this resource is limited by human resource management (HRM) programs, practices, and policies that have a simple operational focus on attracting, selecting, developing, retaining, and utilizing employees to accomplish specified tasks and jobs. Unless HRM is able to reinvent itself to embrace the challenges of the knowledge economy, it will become a constraining factor that undermines a firm's competitiveness rather than a crucial source of competitive advantage.

The competitive demands of today's marketplace require a reorientation of strategic human resource management emphasis that concentrates on building human capital and managing knowledge rather than focusing on primarily matching particular job skills to selected strategies. For example, similar to the ways that firms engage in mass customization of their products, they need to develop corresponding means to accomplish mass customization of the ways in which they manage individual differences within the workforce. Likewise, as firms develop business-to-business partnerships with suppliers and customers, human resource managers must find ways to develop partial employee relationships with those beyond the firm's borders.

It appears that the HRM function in many organizations has become myopic and has directed its attention to efforts to do familiar things better and more efficiently rather than redefining both its role and its contribution to the twenty-first-century organization. The demands of a global, information-based, technology-rich, and quickly changing competitive field require human resource managers to ensure that people truly matter.

Human resource management faces a new imperative in the twenty-first century. It must

- Build strategic capability
- Expand its boundaries
- Manage new roles

It is no longer enough for HRM to maintain a narrow operational focus, view its activities as confined to the boundaries of its own organization, or limit itself only to traditional human resource (HR) responsibilities. To continue as it has in the past will relegate HRM to increasing irrelevance (and likely outsourcing) in the corporation of the future. Although many familiar HRM activities are necessary, they are increasingly distant from a firm's direct value-creating processes. By taking a new perspective on how HRM can create strategic capability and provide value for customers, HR can increase its importance in the twenty-first-century organization.

# Build Strategic Capability

Organizations in the emerging knowledge economy will need to build **strategic capability:** the capacity to create value based on the intangible assets of the firm. [Note: This entire section draws largely on the work of Hubert Saint-Onge (see http://www.knowinc.com/saint-on ge/library/strategic.htm). The **tangible assets** of the firm are well understood: They are readily visible and rigorously quantified; they form an integral part of the balance sheet; they can be easily duplicated; and they depreciate with use. Examples of tangible assets include manufacturing plants, equipment, buildings, and other elements of physical infrastructure. In contrast, **intangible assets** of the firm are less well understood. Intangible assets are invisible, difficult to quantify, not tracked through accounting, must be developed in a path-dependent way over time—they cannot be instantaneously obtained, bought, or imitated—and they appreciate with purposeful use. Examples of intangible assets include technological know-how, customer loyalty, branding, and business processes. Tangible assets are necessary but not sufficient for gaining a competitive advantage in the knowledge economy, because most tangible assets can be imitated or obtained through the market. *It is the intangible assets that will make the difference in which firms succeed and which fail.*

How can you identify whether a firm has strategic capability? Look for these characteristics: a high level of business competency; a superior ability to detect, understand, and direct what's going on in the marketplace (where preferences are shifting rapidly); the ability to transfer skills quickly and accurately across the organization; the ability to scale-up production to meet explosive demand and quickly expand market reach; and the ability to generate new opportunities for the organization before the marketplace has discovered they are required.

*Strategic capability is a readiness for the present and an ability to adapt in the future.*

Strategic capability is obtained through relationships in which the creation, exchange, and harvesting of knowledge build the individual and organizational capabilities required to provide superior value for customers. Strategic capability consists of three components directly related to HR (http://intellectualcapital.org/evolution/main.html,6/2/01): human capital, structural capital, and relationship capital. **Human capital** is the know-how, skills, and capabilities of individuals in an organization. **Human capital** reflects the competencies people bring to their work. Some examples of human capital include technical skills, innovativeness, and leadership competencies. **Structural capital** is the organizational architecture and managerial processes that enable human capital to create market value. Some examples of structural capital include modular and/or cellular structures, information systems, organizational culture, and decision-making processes. **Relationship capital** is the interpersonal connections across members of the firm and relationships with suppliers, customers, and other firms that provide the basis for cooperation and collaborative action. Some examples of relationship capital include trust, consumer loyalty, co-production activities, and licensing agreements (see Table 1.1). The interaction of these three components—human capital, structural capital, and relationship capital—creates value. Human resource management can increase its contribution to a firm's competitiveness by playing a central role in the creation and maintenance of all three components of strategic capability. This can be done through programs, practices, policies, and setting an example in terms of the way the HR unit develops its people, designs itself, and establishes relationships across the organization and beyond its doors.

# Expand Boundaries

When most people think about HRM, they think about hiring, firing, promoting, training, and so forth (the traditional operational focus), and they think about it within the context of a single organization. That is, HRM is thought of as an internal business function. Rarely would anyone think of one company using its HRM programs, practices, and policies on, for example, its suppliers or distributors. Even fewer people would consider the possibility of using a firm's HRM programs, practices, and policies on its customers. Yet, all of these possibilities are a reality in some firms today and will become an imperative for many firms in the growing knowledge economy. Furthermore, by expanding its boundaries beyond the firm to suppliers, distributors, and customers, HRM can have a more significant impact, that is, HRM can make it possible to provide superior value for customers by providing a more rare, important, hard-to-replace-or-imitate, and powerfully leveraged strategic resource. At the most basic level, expanding the boundaries means that HRM professionals use their expertise to help their organization influence the behavior of customers, employees of supplier firms, and individuals in firms that complement or regulate a firm's activities.

Table 1.1 Components of Strategic Capability

| Strategic Capability Component | Definition | Examples | Indicators |
|---|---|---|---|
| Human Capital | • the combined knowledge, skills, and experience of a company's employees—the collective competence and capabilities of a firm's employees | • know-how | • reputation of company employees with head hunters |
| | • "that which goes home with employees at night" | • education | • years of experience in profession |
| | | • vocational qualifications | • rookie ratio (percentage of employees with less than two years experience) |
| | | • work-related knowledge | • employee satisfaction |

| | | | |
|---|---|---|---|
| | • occupational assessments | | • proportion of employees making new idea suggestions (proportion implemented) |
| | • psychometric assessments | | • value added per employee |
| | • work-related competencies | | • value added per salary dollar |
| | • entrepreneurial élan, innovativeness, proactive and reactive abilities, changeability | | |
| Structural Capital | • a firm's organizational capabilities to meet market requirements, such as the organization's routines and structures that support employees' quests for optimum intellectual performance and therefore overall business performance | Intellectual Property | • income per R&D expense |
| | • "that which is left behind when the employee goes home at night" | • patents | • cost of patent maintenance |
| | | • copyrights | • project life-cycle cost per dollar of sales |

- design rights
- trade secrets
- trademarks
- service marks

Infrastructure Assets

- management philosophy
- corporate culture
- management processes
- information systems
- networking systems
- financial relations
- five-year trend of product life cycle

- number of individual computer links to the database
- number of times the database has been consulted
- contributions to the database
- upgrades of the database
- volume of IS use and connections
- cost of IS per sales dollar
- income per dollar of IS expense
- satisfaction with IS expense
- satisfaction with IS service
- ratio of new ideas generated to new ideas implemented
- number of new product introductions
- average length of time for product design and development

| | | | • value of new idea (money saved, money earned) |
|---|---|---|---|
| Relationship Capital | • the networks of strong, cross-cutting personal relationships that provide the basis for collaborative behaviors and cooperative actions | Customer Capital | • growth in business volume |
| | • the organization's relationships or network of associates and their satisfaction with and loyalty to the company—it includes knowledge of market channels, customer and supplier relationships, industry associations and a sound understanding of the impacts of government public policy | • brands | • proportion of sales by repeat customers |
| | • the depth (penetration), width (coverage), and profitability of the organization's franchise | • customers | • brand loyalty |

- customer loyalty
- company names
- backlog orders
- distribution channels
- business collaborations
- licensing agreements
- favorable contracts
- franchising agreements

Social Capital

- dense linkages
- links among people and units
- hierarchy and rank
- network ties

- customer satisfaction
- customer complaints
- product returns as a proportion of sales
- number of supplier/customer alliances and their value
- proportion of customers (suppliers') business that your product (service) represents (in dollar terms)
- sense of community
- disclosive communication
- trust
- collaboration
- informal coordination
- self-organization
- reduced opportunism

- interaction history
- personal & emotional ties
- norms and sanctions
- obligations and expectations
- organizational identity
- interpretations
- shared language and codes
- myths and rituals

Supplier Capital

- bargaining for lower prices
- cooperation on solutions
- J-I-T inventory management

Sources: Jacobs (1965); Stewart (1997); & Strategic Policy Branch, Industry Canada (http://s trategis.ic.gc.ca/SSG/pi00009e.html.) 6/2/01.

## Value Chain

To understand this expanded role for HRM outside its own organization, it is necessary to appreciate the concept of value chains. A **value chain** is a conceptual model of how businesses receive raw materials as input, add value to the raw materials through various processes, and sell finished products to customers. Value chain analysis looks at every step a business goes through, from raw materials to the eventual end-user. The goal is to deliver maximum value for the least possible total cost as quickly as possible.

**Simplified Value Chain Illustration**

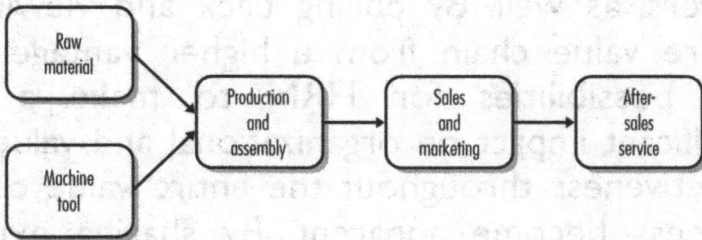

```
  ┌──────────┐
  │   Raw    │
  │ material │──┐
  └──────────┘  │    ┌────────────┐     ┌────────────┐     ┌────────────┐
                ├───▶│ Production  │────▶│   Sales    │────▶│   After-   │
  ┌──────────┐  │    │    and      │     │    and     │     │   sales    │
  │ Machine  │  │    │  assembly   │     │ marketing  │     │  service   │
  │   tool   │──┘    └────────────┘     └────────────┘     └────────────┘
  └──────────┘
```

Networks of suppliers, producers, and distributors can be quite diverse, and the effectiveness of the entire value chain is dependent on coordination and efficiency among them. The quality of relationships between business partners will determine the extent to which value is added for the customers they serve. Thus, weak links in the supply chain, production processes, or distribution chain can dilute the organizational effectiveness of some or all of the participating organizations. If, for example, those who staff an outsourced technical support hotline for a new product have inadequate expertise or surly dispositions, even technologically superior products are likely to suffer declines in market position as this reputation becomes common knowledge.

Traditionally, HRM has focused its attention only on its organizational piece of the value chain. That is, HRM in supplier organizations was distinct and largely unrelated to HRM in the organization that produced the goods or services, and the HRM practiced in distributor or vendor organizations was unrelated to the other two players, as well. By pulling back and viewing the entire value chain from a higher vantage point, the possibilities for HRM to make a more significant impact on organizational and value chain effectiveness throughout the entire value creation process become apparent. By sharing expertise and knowledge and diffusing effective HRM practices throughout the value chain, all of the value chain members can be raised to a higher level of efficiency and effectiveness, and thus the entire value chain as a system can create its own competitive advantage. For example, Shell Services International (SSI), a division of the Royal Dutch/Shell group of companies, provides services to internal operating divisions and external customers around the world. Relationships are governed by service level agreements in which customers contract for specific levels of service that correspond to their unique cost and/or value tradeoffs. Employees on both sides of the agreement need to understand how to make informed decisions, provide effective feedback, and improve performance to make the most of the transaction. Human resource expertise in performance appraisal, negotiation processes, and decision-making tools could be beneficial for SSI and its customers.

In the past, a business culture of not sharing information, knowledge, or expertise with other organizations prevented companies from reaping the benefits of this broader perspective on the boundaries of HRM. "We pay our HR people to do our HR; You get your own" describes this narrowly focused mind-set. As Fred Adair, former president of change management consultancy Smythe-Dorward-Lambert, says, "It has proven very difficult for companies in adjacent links of the supply chain to share data and trust that others will play fair. While it's often clear that sharing and collaboration can have large benefits, people suspect the other guy is getting more. Those who are successful in joining forces, however, can develop incredible momentum, because the good news about increased efficiency travels quickly up and down the chain" (Fahrenwald, Wise, & Glynn, 2001).

It is no longer desirable or even feasible to maintain a narrow perspective on organizational boundaries or to treat businesses with which you have relationships with automatic mistrust. Borders between suppliers, competitors, and customers have, in fact, become blurred. For example, Motorola executives found that in one of their alliances with Intel, they were a supplier; in another setting, they were rivals; and in still another relationship, they were a customer (Ulrich, 1997). Another example also illustrates this point. In a process called **collaborative design,** product development teams from several departments at different companies, using the Internet, can view the same blueprint simultaneously and make changes on the blueprint that are visible to all. This saves the time and cost of faxing or mailing drawings with each new change to each company. In this way, the Internet has created permeable organizational boundaries (Totty, 2001). These permeable organizational boundaries have direct and indirect implications for HRM. When employees from different companies are working on the same product over the Internet, how do you manage them and which firm's HR policies shape the relationship? How do you assess the relative value of the intellectual contributions from diverse firms? How do you facilitate their ability to coordinate efforts that will benefit all of the organizations involved? How do you maintain the security of each firm's trade secrets?

## Customer Human Resource Management

A customer orientation in HRM has typically emphasized its internal customers, that is, the employees who enable the firm to create value for the external customer and thus enhance organizational performance and profitability. However, HR practices can enhance competitive advantage and organizational performance by enabling the external customer—the individual or institution that purchases a firm's goods or services—to contribute directly to organizational activities and outcomes (Lengnick-Hall & Lengnick-Hall, 1999). This goal can be achieved in several ways: (1) using HRM to guide customer behavior for the benefit of both the customer and the organization; (2) using HRM to facilitate the inclusion of customers in the creation and distribution of products and services; (3) using customers as organizational auditors, providing feedback on what practices to start, stop, or continue; and (4) using customers as quasi HR managers who directly participate in the management of employees.

First, HRM can guide customer behavior for the benefit of both the customer and the organization. For example, if a skating rink provides clear rules for safe and considerate behavior (analogous to performance expectations or job descriptions for customers), its customers are more likely to behave in courteous ways and create an enjoyable atmosphere for other customers. As another example, when fast food restaurants provide clear expectations for customers to throw away their own trash and make it easy for customers to comply, the dining experience is better for all customers. By providing effective training and work process information for customers, the customers themselves enhance the organization's effectiveness. Thus, courteous customers beget more customers and increase an organization's revenues.

Second, customers can participate as team members who actually help produce and deliver a product or service. For example, customers who buy computers via the Internet receive their computers in component parts with "some assembly required." To be an effective co-producer, the customer must know how to assemble the computer and make it usable. The company must therefore provide training and skill development to its customers (through printed instructions, videos, online help, and so on) to enable them to finish the production process. So, for example, HRM can assist in developing tools such as training manuals and performance assessment checklists for customers that parallel the type of developmental resources HRM has traditionally provided for employees. Effective HRM for customers both makes the customers more competent users of the firm's products or services and enhances the customers' satisfaction with those products or services.

Third, customers can serve as auditors, determining whether confidence can be placed in the perceived value of the goods or services produced. Many restaurants and other service organizations use customer feedback mechanisms (for example, customer comment cards) to obtain information about what works well and what needs attention. Raytheon Aircraft uses a similar, but more sophisticated, approach with their customer "walk-through" program. Raytheon recognizes that many purchasers of personal aircraft are greatly concerned about manufacturing quality but lack the technical expertise to evaluate this directly. Therefore, Raytheon encourages potential customers of their Beechcraft planes to tour the factory and observe the manufacturing process. Internal HRM programs, practices, and policies have focused on ensuring that manufacturing employees visibly demonstrate confidence, expertise, care with details, and professionalism. Raytheon believes that when customers observe the caliber of their employees at work, they will be more likely to purchase a Beechcraft plane than a competitor's aircraft. As auditors, customers help ensure that the reputation of Raytheon's products remains positive. Their feedback from these walk-throughs provides the company with needed information on what practices they should continue, which need to be terminated, and what new practices need to be implemented to ensure customer satisfaction.

And fourth, customers can serve as quasi HR managers and tailor their own treatment by an organization to meet their specific needs. For example, Ritz-Carlton Hotels have a policy that empowers every employee to resolve a guest's problem and to prevent a repeat occurrence (Berry, 1995). Therefore, customers can have their needs met quickly and satisfactorily by any member of the hotel's staff. Since many customers have idiosyncratic needs, customers, in effect, become HR managers in charge of their own ad hoc employees in an effort to accomplish the necessary work.

In summary, expanding boundaries means looking beyond traditional ways of defining where HRM takes place and whom it affects. Consideration of the entire value chain opens up new possibilities for applying HRM programs, practices, and policies in ways that enhance the efficiency and effectiveness of the entire system. When the entire system of suppliers, manufacturers, and distributors is viewed as one large quasi organization, improvement of the whole can reap benefits for each of the individual components, too. Furthermore, expanding boundaries to include customers as well as employees creates new opportunities for utilizing people who aren't typically viewed as part of a firm's HR. Capitalizing on opportunities to apply HRM in new and creative ways will be a key competency for effectively managing HR in the new knowledge economy.

# Manage New Roles

Many of the limiting assumptions and narrow perspectives on the role of HRM in organizations are a holdover from its origins as an "employment bureaucracy" (Jacoby, 1985). Human resource management developed into a bureaucracy as a result of attempts by employers in the early 1900s to stabilize employment. At the time, there was a growing hostility between employers and workers that often resulted in strikes and acts of violence. Furthermore, waste and inefficiency reached intolerable levels. Through the creation of an array of impersonal, rule-bound procedures to regulate the treatment of workers, employers hoped to use HRM to reduce conflict and manage employees for maximum efficiency (Kaufman, 2000).

In the early 1900s, employers adopted these bureaucratic procedures as a way to regulate themselves. Later, in the 1930s, employers further bureaucratized the HRM function in response to legislation that favored the establishment and protection of labor unions. Additional employment legislation was introduced from the 1960s through the 1990s (such as the Civil Rights Act of 1964), creating more need for bureaucratization. By the end of the twentieth century, forms, paperwork, and compliance activities occupied much of the time of HR departments.

A bureaucratic view persists today, both inside and outside of the HR profession, which sees HRM as a set of discrete practices organized around a set of specific functions. From this perspective, the role of HRM is to attract and select qualified job applicants, to develop performance management and compensation systems that align employee behaviors with organizational goals, and to assist in the development and retention of a diverse work force to meet current and future organizational requirements (Huselid, 1997). Specific areas of responsibility for HRM include: job and organizational design, recruitment and selection, performance management, compensation and benefits, employee development and training, HR planning, labor relations, diversity management, and compliance with legal and governmental guidelines (Huselid, 1997). In fact, to become a certified HR professional, the Society for Human Resource Management (SHRM) requires competency testing and job experience in all of these areas. Consequently, HRM has evolved into a highly efficient employment bureaucracy with a clearly defined body of knowledge and accepted practices.

Although a narrow, functionalist perspective of HRM served organizations well during the industrial era, it will not serve organizations as well in the knowledge economy. This is not to say that organizations will no longer perform traditional HRM functional activities—they will continue to do so. However, to manage HR in the future, HRM will also have to adopt new roles to address new challenges.

Staying within the functional bureaucratic boxes that HRM has created for itself will only undervalue its impact on organizational effectiveness. Failure to change with the demands of the new economy will mean that formal HRM will become less important, whereas such new challenges as knowledge management and human capital management will be absorbed elsewhere within the organization (Saint-Onge, 2001). But this does not have to happen. In fact, HR is the logical source for solutions to these new challenges. However, to become part of the solution rather than a constraint on competitiveness, HRM must break out of its bureaucratic past. This will require a shift in its paradigm from functions and processes to roles.

What is a role? A **role** represents responsibilities, relationships, and areas of contribution. It is also a set of expectations. It is a general construct that does not specify means or activities. In this way, a role is analogous to an organization's vision statement. The vision statement of an organization identifies a general direction for the organization to pursue, such as Microsoft's "empower people through great software anytime, anyplace, and on any device." Notice the means to achieve the vision are not specified. As a consequence, the vision statement orients organizational members toward desired goals, yet allows them to determine what must be done, as well as how to do it, and to change their actions as the situation evolves. A role for HRM serves a purpose similar to an organization's vision statement. It orients HR professionals to move in a desired direction—and identifies responsibilities, relationships, areas of contribution, and expectations—without locking HRM into specific methods and techniques.

Why manage roles? The answer is simple. By managing roles, HRM is freed from the functional shackles of the past and allowed to make value-added contributions to the success of the organization. The HRM paradigm thereby changes from functions and processes to outcomes and accomplishments. For example, managing a role such as "knowledge facilitator" (to be explained more thoroughly in the next chapter) means more than the traditional HRM view of training and development. It is an organizational role focused on learning—one that helps the entire enterprise acquire new knowledge and use that knowledge to continuously adapt to changing environments. When viewed as a role to manage, such as knowledge facilitator, HR professionals may use many different methods, only one of which is training and development, to ensure organizational learning capabilities. For example, as a knowledge facilitator, HR professionals can play an active part in the development and management of the information technology system of the organization, even to the extent of developing applications to accumulate, store, and disseminate what individual employees learn.

Just as expanding boundaries opens up new opportunities for HRM to influence other organizations in a "business ecosystem"—and thus make more value-added contributions to business success—managing roles expands the methods and processes available to HRM for meeting new challenges. Consequently, looking at HRM through the lens of roles means that HR professionals have a larger arsenal to deploy in the interest of the organization.

What roles should HRM play in the knowledge economy? The answer to this question requires an examination of characteristics of the new economic context. The next chapter will describe those characteristics and propose four new roles for HRM. Then, each of those four roles will be described in detail in the following chapters.

## Summary

By the end of the twentieth century, some people questioned whether HRM made any value-added contributions to organizations. Many of the traditional administrative HR functions had become automated processes most efficiently outsourced to organizations with specialized expertise. This view was most sarcastically expressed by *Fortune* magazine business writer

Thomas Stewart (1997): "Nestling warm and sleepy in your company, like the asp in Cleopatra's bosom, is a department whose employees spend 80% of their time on routine administrative tasks. Nearly every function of this department can be performed more expertly for less by others. Chances are its leaders are unable to describe their contribution to value added except in trendy, unquantifiable, and wannabe terms—yet, like a serpent unaffected by its own venom, the department frequently dispenses to others advice on how to eliminate work that does not add value" (Stewart, 1997).

Human resource management is at a crossroad in its evolution. It has developed highly efficient programs, practices, and policies to serve industrial organizations of the twentieth century. However, the demands of the knowledge economy require from HRM more than an efficient employment bureaucracy. To become a viable contributor to organizations in the new economy, HRM must undergo self-examination and redirection. This will require a new focus: on building strategic capability (a readiness for the present and an ability to adapt in the future; on expanding the boundaries of HRM to include the entire value chain), including suppliers, distributors, and customers; and on managing new roles—roles that expand the methods and processes of HRM. The challenges are formidable.

# Chapter 2

# Human Resource Management in the Knowledge Economy

"Knowledge is the most democratic source of power."
—Alvin Toffler

"I don't believe evolution is about survival of the fittest. I believe it is about survival of the most useful."
—John Woods

What is the knowledge economy? The knowledge economy encompasses all jobs, companies, and industries in which the knowledge and capabilities of people, rather than the capabilities of machines or technologies, determines competitive advantage. Of the 19.5 million jobs that are projected to be created in the United States from 1998 to 2008, 19.1 million of them will be in the service sector (Hecker, 2001). From retail sales to computers to biotechnology, these jobs will be more knowledge-intensive in their demands on workers and organizations. Although the service sector is an obvious place to find more knowledge-intensive work, the manufacturing sector is also becoming more dependent on knowledge and human capabilities as microprocessors and computers pervade almost every facet of work.

The knowledge economy came into existence as a result of the commercialization of information and communication technologies—what is collectively known as *information technology* (Burton-Jones, 1999). The rapid development of computers and microprocessors has made it possible to collect and use vast amounts of information from a variety of sources in a more integrative and interactive manner than ever before. Networking and connectivity, coupled with the Internet, have made it possible for information to be acquired and shared globally, so that proximity no longer determines the ability of people to work together collaboratively. Combined, these forces have dramatically altered business and everyday life.

In this information-intensive economy, competitive advantage is based primarily on the application of knowledge, and not all of the data, intelligence, and wisdom with which a global company needs to compete can be found in one place (Doz, Santos, & Williamson, 2001). Increasingly, knowledge is dispersed around the world. Furthermore, the cost of overcoming distance is falling rapidly for commodities that are mobile, such as capital, goods, and information. Consequently, these commodities are readily accessible to firms that previously faced limitations because of their geographic location.

Knowledge, rather than the concrete characteristics of goods or services or the mechanics of production processes, is becoming the defining characteristic of economic activities. The impact of knowledge is pervasive in both the "old economy" as well as the "new economy." Human know-how is a crucial component in virtually everything we produce, and it determines how we produce valued goods and services. As Don Tapscott (1996) asserts, more added value is created by brain than brawn.

Many agricultural and industrial jobs are becoming knowledge work. Already, almost 60% of all American workers are knowledge workers and eight of ten new jobs are in information-intensive sectors of the economy. The factory of today is as different from the industrial factory of the old economy as the old factory from the craft production that preceded it. Farms are operated with agricultural equipment brimming from chips. Cargo is shipped in containers loaded by giant computer-controlled cranes or in jumbo jets loaded with software.

The knowledge economy is about adding ideas to products and turning new ideas into new products. Tapscott provides a vivid illustration.

There are smart clothes with chips in the collar; smart vehicles brimming with microprocessors that do a hundred new things every year; smart maps that tell a trucker's location and automatically change tire pressure according to the weather and road conditions; smart radios that store the traffic report for you when you want it; smart houses that manage energy, protect you from intrusion, and run a bath for you before you arrive; smart elevators that phone in when they're getting sick; and smart greeting cards that sing to you.

Products like those described by Tapscott have six key attributes that distinguish them from products that were available in the past. These attributes are the following (Botkin, 1999).

1. *They learn.* The more you use them, the smarter they get. The more you use them, the smarter you get, too. For example, some word processing programs create customized dictionaries and automatically correct spelling errors.

2. *They improve with use.* They are enhanced, rather than depleted, when used. They grow up instead of being used up. Internet banking, for example, can be customized

over time to reflect a patron's transaction patterns.

3.  *They anticipate.* They know what you want; they recommend what you might want next. Grocery scanners use the customer's current basket of goods to automatically generate coupons on the back of receipts to stimulate future sales.

4.  *They are interactive.* There is two-way communication between you and them. Hardcorps Sports sells a ski jacket woven with a genetically engineered "phase change material" developed by Outlast Inc., which turns warmer when the skier is cold and automatically cools down if the slopes are sunny.

5.  *They remember.* They record and recall your past actions to develop a profile. Nearly every Internet sales operation has sophisticated customer profile systems to encourage related purchases.

6.  *They are customized.* They are uniquely configured to your individual specifications—in real time—at no additional cost. Injection devices for diabetics can adjust insulin dosages to respond to current blood sugar levels and activity levels.

The knowledge economy has even spawned a new type of global, knowledge-based organization, labeled a "metanational" by Doz, Santos, and Williamson (2001). In contrast to global organizations that view the world as a single, fairly homogeneous market, or multinationals that see each country as a distinct segment, these metanational organizations view the world as a global canvas dotted with pockets of technology, market intelligence, and capabilities. Thus, metanationals are able to capitalize on the synergies of global commonalities while adapting to specialized opportunities generated by local capabilities. Metanationals see untapped potential in these pockets of specialist knowledge that are scattered around the world. And, by sensing and mobilizing this dispersed knowledge, metanationals are able to innovate more effectively than their rivals. Rather than promoting a universal set of products that are globally competitive, metanationals weave together a tapestry of many local specialized capabilities to create local customization with global reach.

The complexity of this type of organization requires extensive knowledge management at all levels to achieve what Bartlett and Ghoshal (1993) refer to as "distributed entrepreneurship." Bartlett and Ghoshal argue that this explains why Asea Brown Boveri (ABB), an electrotechnical firm with worldwide operations, has turned the conventional design of its HR activities inside out to achieve radical decentralization. In ABB, frontline managers are responsible for creating and pursuing opportunities, whereas midlevel managers review and develop supporting initiatives and top management establishes a strategic mission and supporting standards. Consequently, the corporate HR staff consists of a single manager, since employees are recruited and developed at the level of the frontline business operations, and the managers of entrepreneurial business units have wide discretion in the size, scope, and allocation of HR activities.

To sum up, knowledge is becoming the primary component of virtually all products, services, and work activities. The effective production, accumulation, and handling of knowledge are becoming key sources of competitive advantage distinguishing businesses, industries, and nations. How has the knowledge economy changed the way business is conducted? We will address that issue next.

# What's Different in the Knowledge Economy?

Numerous researchers, consultants, and authors have attempted to capture the key factors that distinguish the knowledge economy. However, since there is no universal agreement on specific characteristics that distinguish knowledge-based competition from other economic forms, this is a challenging task. Furthermore, there is no universal agreement on terminology. New concepts have necessitated new jargon, and some of it is more descriptive and widely accepted than others. Table 2.1 summarizes eleven characteristics of the knowledge economy that have been proposed by some of the leading thinkers on this topic.

First, the knowledge economy uses technology to create symbolic goods (Burton-Jones, 1999). Electronic symbols represent information that we need to know about physical goods to conduct business, such as a banking transaction. These electronic symbols—ones and zeros—digitize human communication, the delivery of government programs, the execution of health care, and business transactions (Tapscott, 1996). Furthermore, electronic symbols can be transmitted and received instantaneously and worldwide. Thus, a firm's knowledge resources must include the ability to create and manage these symbols.

Second, the knowledge economy places comparatively little reliance on the need for physical concentration or massing of labor, materials, and money. Previously, it was necessary to co-locate these resources in order to produce goods and services. Now, the same efficiencies can be realized through what one author calls "demassification" (Burton-Jones, 1999). Labor, materials, and money can be combined from locations dispersed across the globe. Programmers in India and California, for example, can simultaneously work on developing the same software program. This means a firm must be able to manage a workplace that is dispersed and does not provide the same kind of embedded structure associated with physical proximity and plant layout common in the industrial economy.

Table 2.1  Eleven Characteristics of the Knowledge Economy

| Knowledge Economy Characteristic | Definition |
| --- | --- |
| Symbolic goods/ Digitization | Electronic symbols representing information about the physical goods that we need to know to conduct the transactions (for example, details of a banking transaction): human communication, delivery of government programs, execution of health care, business transactions all become based on ones and zeros. |
| Demassification | Reduced dependency on the need for physical concentration or massing (co-location) of labor, materials, and money. |
| Boundaryless enterprise/ Globalization | Knowledge transcends firm, industry, and national boundaries; organizations have time- and space-independence; work can be performed from a variety of locations. |
| Virtualization | Physical things can become virtual, such as corporations, teams, auction sites, and so on. |
| Connectedness/ Unprecedented partnering/ Integration-internetworking | Interconnections within and between organizations and institutions; interconnections between businesses and customers; no one organization can have all the knowledge needed, so partnering is essential. |
| Disintermediation | Elimination of the intermediaries in economic activity—anything that stands between producers and consumers. |
| Convergence | Bringing together different economic sectors to create new products and services (for example, telecommunications). |
| Personalization/ Mass customization/ Prosumption | Fitting products and services to the unique needs of individual customers; consumers become involved in the actual production process as their knowledge, information, and ideas become part of the product specification process. |
| Dynamic pricing | Pricing decisions change based on time and place as products and services are constantly updated and shifted. |
| Immediacy | Business is transacted in real time; enterprises continuously and immediately adjust to changing business conditions; product life cycles become shorter. |
| Customer communities | Customers talk with other customers on a local and global scale (for example, Amazon.com). |

Sources: *Tapscott (1996); Burton-Jones (1999); Baird & Henderson (2001)*

Third, the knowledge economy has no defined boundaries (Burton-Jones, 1999; Tapscott,

1996). Knowledge transcends firm, industry, and even national borders. Needed knowledge resides in no single place. Organizations have both time- and space-independence, so work can be performed from a variety of locations. The proliferation of PalmPilots™, laptops, and other connectivity technologies everywhere, from the airport to the restaurant to the automobile, attests to the portability of work. This means that firms must be able to manage workflows that take place 24/7/365.

Fourth, technology makes it possible to transform physical entities into virtual ones. A virtual corporation is one without walls and without permanent employees. It relies on contractual relationships with suppliers and distributors, and it has a contingent workforce (Cortada & Woods, 1999). Teams can be assembled from all over the world and can work together without having to be in the same location at the same time. Virtualization offers benefits of increased flexibility and breadth of resources but also introduces complicated challenges in terms of coordination and maintaining consistent purposes.

Fifth, computers and the Internet make it possible for organizations and institutions to become increasingly interconnected. Information can be shared and ad hoc partnerships can be created and dissolved to meet situational needs. This "unprecedented partnering" is necessitated by the fact that no single organization can have all of the knowledge it needs to compete successfully (Botkin, 1999). Consequently, firms must develop new skills for knowledge management activities that capitalize on their expanded reach. Businesses are more interconnected with their customers in ways not possible in the past. Relationship marketing and individually targeted advertising create a uniquely "personal" impersonal relationship. It is now unusual, for example, to make a catalog purchase without being asked for your email address, so that the company can keep a customer posted on upcoming specials and new products. This suggests that the talent pool for an organization is likely to include customers and employees of the firms providing raw materials and the firm's own human resources.

Sixth, the middleman is (mostly) eliminated in business transactions between an organization and its customers as well as between an organization and its employees. Tapscott calls this factor "disintermediation." It is the elimination of anything that stands between producers and consumers. The erosion of travel agencies, full-service gas stations, financial service intermediaries, and similar transaction roles illustrates this trend. This phenomenon is also occurring in HR as more organizations, such as Dell Computer Corporation, adopt electronic HR delivery systems. These delivery systems allow employees and managers to get what they need when they need it (and without using an HR middleman). Activities that merely transmit information or transfer objects from one location to another are particularly vulnerable. Disintermediation underscores the need to add considerable value in order to maintain viability in the emerging knowledge economy and to ensure that this contribution is well recognized.

Seventh, the knowledge economy brings together different economic sectors that in the past functioned as separate entities. Boundaries between industries, organizations, units, and technologies are becoming blurred. For example, the telecommunications industry is a combination of the old telephone industry with television, computers, and content providers. This convergence has yielded such products as "smart telephones," which can be used for talking, reading email, surfing the Internet, and so on. These fluid boundaries place a premium on the ability to continuously learn, unlearn, and relearn at all organizational levels. The knowledge economy is also introducing new areas of competition among economic sectors. Rivalry is not limited to product functionality but can focus, as well, on the basic nature of the solution being offered. Consider, for example, the contest currently taking place between personal computer and microprocessor allies (such as IBM and Compaq), who intend to maintain power on the desktop, and interface firms (such as Oracle and Sun Microsystems), who intend to move computing power to the network. Redefined solutions mean that firms will need to be able to quickly and efficiently develop new capabilities.

Eighth, the knowledge economy increasingly operates to provide tailored products and services that meet the unique needs of individual customers. Termed "personalization," "mass consumption," or "prosumption," they all refer to consumers taking an active role in the production process as their knowledge, information, and ideas become part of the product specification process (Baird & Henderson, 2001; Botkin, 1999; Tapscott, 1996). As a case in point, Dell Computer Corporation has pioneered mass customization in the personal computer manufacturing industry. Along with this, the lines between products and services are becoming quite fuzzy as firms increasingly bundle services with their tangible products (that is, information hotlines for everything from cookbooks to clothing to appliances to computers) and service businesses make efforts to provide some form of tangible deliverable with their services (that is, hardbound financial portfolio displays or frequent user cards for many types of retail outlets). Consequently, organizations need to be able to continuously augment their creative capabilities and capacity for innovation.

Ninth, in the knowledge economy, pricing becomes more dynamic (Baird & Henderson, 2001). That is, pricing decisions change based on time and place, since products and services are constantly updated and shifted. Prices, like products, can be tailored to individual customers. In addition, technology advances make it easy, quick, and inexpensive to comparison shop in virtual space. Moreover, the firms whose products and services are being compared have much less control over the process than ever before. As a result, firms will need to develop new ways to influence consumer behavior that rely on loose ties and building relationships rather than on conventional advertising and special pricing policies.

Tenth, in the knowledge economy, business is often transacted in real time, that is, there are no delays between steps in the process. Successful companies continuously adjust to changing business conditions, and they can do so immediately. Aircraft manufacturers that have implemented enterprise resource planning systems, for example, automatically initiate the production of components in their supplier's factory when an order is placed for a plane. Furthermore, product life cycles have become much shorter. Firms such as Intel routinely invest in the manufacturing capabilities that enable them to scale up production at the same time they are working on the technology breakthroughs that will create the next generation microprocessor. Oftentimes it feels like businesses are running the fast-forward button on a videotape player. The speed of action in the knowledge economy means that firms must be agile, resourceful, and adept at interpreting events and making sense of the environment "on the fly."

Finally, the knowledge economy has created customer communities. Customers can talk with other customers on local and global bases. They can talk and share information and do so in real time. Reactions from other consumers are readily available to evaluate products and services as diverse as videos and movies, national parks, restaurants, and automobiles. Thus, knowledge sharing takes place both among organizations and among customers. This means that firms must learn how to influence individuals and ideas in their environment with greater adeptness and subtlety than ever before.

All in all, the knowledge economy has a multitude of characteristics that present new challenges for businesses. Gone are the days of "slack" (periods of time between processes within a firm, or periods of time between steps in transactions outside of the firm). Slack was often achieved by maintaining large inventories of raw materials and finished products to accommodate unpredictable fluctuations in demand. Furthermore, Henry Ford's mass production technology, which could produce lots of cars efficiently (as long as they were all the same kind) has given way to mass customization technologies that are so sophisticated that they can provide individually tailored products and services with the same or better efficiency as standardized production processes. Globalization is more than a meaningless buzz word; markets for products, services, and labor are truly international. People can work at home, organizations can exist in virtual reality, and industries can be converged in ways never before dreamed possible. Finally, the pace of change has become fast, very fast.

# How Do Organizations Compete in the Knowledge Economy?

Winners in the knowledge economy will have to outdistance their competitors on three different levels (Doz, Santos, & Williamson, 2001):

1. Competing on the sensing plane
2. Competing on the mobilizing plane
3. Competing on the operating plane

At the highest level, organizations will have to constantly search out knowledge that could lead to the development of new products and services. They must do this by identifying sources of relevant technologies, competencies, and understanding about leading-edge customers. Of course, other organizations will be doing the same thing, so a real premium will be placed on finding that knowledge that others don't discover or on being able to interpret the vast array of available data more accurately, more insightfully, and more quickly than others. Organizations need the ability that hockey star Wayne Gretzky had: not skating to where the hockey puck is but skating to where it will be (Huang, 1998). This level of competition is called "competing on the sensing plane," and is much like prospecting: It requires such competencies as reconnaissance and discovery. Competing on the sensing plane enables organizations to create the future.

Once useable knowledge is discovered, it must be mobilized to create a product or service. Doz, Santos, and Williamson (2001) suggest that firms create "magnets," which are organizational structures that attract knowledge from different parts of the corporation (and sometimes with the help of customers) to central locations, where it can be integrated and applied. To achieve this, firms must have core competencies (integrated knowledge sets within an organization that distinguish it from its competitors and deliver value to customers) to provide an effective basis for selection and assimilation (Bohlander, Snell, & Sherman, 2001).

Pioneering new products and services requires innovation. Creative capabilities are needed to quickly develop the products, processes, and services that customers want at a competitive price; to find new solutions to old problems; and to adapt familiar solutions to changing circumstances (Huang, 1998). This level of competition is called "competing on the mobilizing plane" and requires, among others, entrepreneurship and mobilization competencies.

Finally, in the knowledge economy, as in the old economy, knowledge must be operationalized to create and distribute the products or services. This more traditional level of competition is evermore fierce as organizations look for efficiencies throughout their entire value chains. Linkages among suppliers, distributors, customers, and other institutions are crucial for eliminating non – value-adding steps. This level of competition is called "competing on the operating plane" and requires, among other factors, efficiency and flexibility competencies.

Together, the competencies necessary to compete effectively in the knowledge economy constitute what Dave Ulrich (1997) calls "organizational capabilities." Organizational capabilities are the DNA of competitiveness. Just as an individual blessed with good DNA (for example, intelligence and athleticism) has a potential advantage in life, that advantage must be realized through development, application, and opportunity. The same is true for organizational capabilities. Having the capabilities is a necessary, but not sufficient, condition for success. Organizations must also be able to develop those capabilities, apply them, and match them to opportunities.

To sum up, competition in the knowledge economy requires succeeding on three levels: sensing, mobilizing, and operationalizing. Different competencies are needed for different levels of competition. The combination of competencies needed for succeeding across all three levels is collectively known as "organizational capabilities."

Human resource management plays a significant role in creating and developing the organizational capabilities needed for competing in the knowledge economy.

# Human Resource Management's Opportunity in the Knowledge Economy

Don Tapscott (1996: 260) argues that "the human resources function in general, and human resource professionals in particular, should be uniquely positioned to provide leadership for the transformation of the enterprise." However, rather than being an agent of change and adaptation, the HR function is too often slow to respond. As Tapscott notes, "Although some human resource professionals are rising to the challenge, too many are not. The basic problem is that in the first era, human resource professionals were mere suppliers of human resource functions, such as staffing needs and compensation planning. This may have made a lot of sense during a period of stability and steady growth. But as we move into the digital economy, the human resource profession needs to reinvent itself and forge partnerships with others in the organization for the transformation of the corporation."

How should HRM adapt to the knowledge economy? Ulrich (1999) poses three questions that are useful for addressing this issue.

- What is HRM work?
- Who does HRM work?
- How will technology change the HRM function?

## What Is Human Resource Management Work?

In the knowledge economy, HRM work will not be confined to its conventional functions of staffing, training and development, performance management, and so on. Human resource management work in the knowledge economy includes both activities that overlap with other traditional business functions (for instance, finance, marketing, strategy) and some that are nontraditional (for instance, knowledge management). For this reason, HRM is no longer simply focused on "managing people" in the conventional meaning of the phrase. Human resource management is now responsible for managing the capabilities that people create and the relationships that people must develop.

## Who Does Human Resource Management Work?

HR professionals still do much of the traditional HR work, although some of that work has been outsourced (staffing, benefits, and so on) or digitized (for example, electronic HR). Furthermore, a substantial portion of conventional HRM work is now being done by line managers and professionals from other fields, such as information technology, or in other parts of the organization, such as the entrepreneurial units of ABB mentioned previously. In the knowledge economy, as HRM work expands, responsibility for HR will truly be jointly shared among HR managers, employees, and external vendors.

## How Will Technology Change the Human Resource Management Function?

By increasing administrative efficiency, technology allows HR to have fewer staff making more value-added contributions to their organizations. The rapid evolution of electronic-HR delivery systems is pushing more information in more usable formats to employees and managers who can use it directly for the benefit of their organizations. In terms of conventional transactions, HR is being disintermediated. However, technology promises to impact HR in ways far beyond simply automating clerical activities.

Twenty-one HR systems professionals have identified the following technology trends affecting HR that are in various stages of becoming realities (Boyett et al., 2001).

1.  *Fast and cheap access to accurate real time HR information.* Access and the ability to analyze, assess, interpret, manipulate, leverage, and share the information effectively will be key to giving organizations a strategic edge. Successful data mining will be made possible by the use of data warehouses with their ability to consolidate internal and external information with powerful analytical tools.

2.  *Ubiquitous access to information to improve employee effectiveness and efficiency.* This means working from anywhere and at anytime. The size, format, and footprint of technology deliverables will move from departmental desktop devices operating under the full control of the user organization to a mixture of hand-held, pocket-sized, integrated devices and wireless linkages that provide needed access on a real time basis to centralized processing and data storage capabilities. Instant access to

all needed knowledge and to essential meaningful data will be a keystone for the successful enterprise.

3. *A variety of analytics and decision trees.* These expert systems will "walk" managers through every step of a decision about people issues. The information the manager receives at each step in the decision process will vary depending on his or her answers to previous questions and will provide the manager with estimates of the risks associated with each alternative. In familiar and somewhat predictable environments, analytical systems will provide "predictor" algorithms that help anticipate and forecast possible problems, such as turnover, recruitment, pay, and employee relations down to the individual employee level. For more chaotic settings, what-if scenarios will provide virtual reality simulations that will enable managers to try out ideas and test different courses of action to make better people decisions.

4. *Smart self-service.* This is self-service expanding to communicate through smart phones and handheld personal data assistants (PDAs). Much of the new Web self-service will reduce the need for call centers and most employee self-service will be entirely

Web-based. In addition, natural language speech recognition enables intuitive application to be implemented, and while speech recognition is in the early stages of acceptance, it will be a factor in twenty-first-century self-service. For both employee and manager, self-service will have to be more intuitive than ever. This will include push and pull technology, content that is filtered and relevant for the person in the role(s) they are performing and event driven, as well.

5. *Customized content.* Human resource management systems in the twenty-first century will enable employees to perform optimally by providing knowledgeable content that has been filtered based on the employee's role(s) in the organization. The vendors of the future will provide not only the transactional systems necessary for this infrastructure but they will also become the "aggregators" of content for their customers and provide a wide range of hosting as the demand for better, faster, and cheaper technology support prevails.

# Why Human Resource Management Roles?

Much current thinking in HRM suggests that its practices must be integrated around common themes (Ulrich, 1999). We propose that HRM roles can provide a logical basis for constructing common themes that support an organization's ability to adapt to the demands of the knowledge economy. Moreover, we propose that HRM roles should encompass more than HRM practices. Indeed, whatever it takes, even stepping outside of traditional HRM activities: That is what the HRM function should be doing to contribute to organizational effectiveness. Roles provide more flexibility than functions. Roles reduce rigid functional boundaries and facilitate adaptation and adjustment. What roles should HRM assume in the knowledge economy? We discuss next the HR roles that will be needed.

# New Roles and New Challenges for Human Resource Management

To effectively compete in the knowledge economy, organizations will need HRM that is role-based (that is, not tied to specific functional responsibilities, as in the past) and contributes directly to the creation of organizational capabilities. Four roles are identified that make it possible to create those needed capabilities: *human capital steward, knowledge facilitator, relationship builder,* and *rapid deployment specialist* (see Table 2.2).

# Human Capital Steward

A recent *Business Week* article proclaims "The turn of the millennium is a turn from hamburgers to software. Software is an idea; hamburger is a cow. There will still be hamburger makers in the twenty-first century, of course, but the power, prestige, and money will flow to companies with indispensable intellectual property" (Coy, 2000). Later, the article proposes,

> In the Creative Economy, the most important intellectual property isn't software or music or movies. It's the stuff inside employees' heads. When assets were physical things like coal mines, shareholders truly owned them. But when the vital assets are people, there can be no true ownership (by anyone other than the individual employee). *The best that corporations can do is to create an environment that makes the best people want to stay.*

Human capital is the knowledge, skills, abilities, and experience unique to an individual employee. The collective human capital of all of an organization's employees forms a unique resource that distinguishes it from other organizations and provides the basis for other forms of competitive advantage. The new role of human capital steward requires accumulating, concentrating, conserving, complementing, and recovering the collective knowledge, skills, and abilities within an organization (Hamel & Prahalad, 1993). To keep up in the knowledge economy, organizations will need to develop a deep reservoir of talent among employees and free agents. Human resource management professionals must develop competencies and commitment among employees. The role of HR will focus on keeping the best minds and thinkers engaged.

Table 2.2 New Roles and New Challenges for Human Resource Management in the Knowledge Economy

| New Roles for HRM | New Challenges for HRM |
| --- | --- |
| Human Capital Steward | • Intellectual capital is not owned by the employer but is bought and sold in human capital markets.<br><br>• Workers are volunteers or free agents.<br><br>• Market contracts replace (most) employment contracts.<br><br>• HRM must ensure that the organization's human capital is available, capable, effective, and grows in value.<br><br>• HRM must broker HR services, such as talent acquisition, learning, and so forth.<br><br>• HRM must leverage human capital (that is, focus on doing the right things and gaining maximum output for a given input). |

- There is a greater dependence on key knowledge workers and ensuring they are attracted and retained.

- There will be higher entry-level requirements for employment.

- Careers replace jobs.

Knowledge Facilitator
- There is an increased emphasis on learning and encouraging people to learn continuously.

- There is a necessity to manage knowledge (acquisition, dissemination, and so forth).

- The organization must tap into all employees' knowledge as sources of innovation.

- HRM must facilitate the sharing of knowledge acquired by employees.

- HRM must determine how to reward knowledge acquisition and sharing.

- Information must be made available and accessible to employees.

- Firms must act on the new knowledge and insights, and abandon obsolete behaviors.

Relationship Builder
- There is an increased emphasis on cross-functional teamwork.

- Technology will make information more accessible and will join people together in different ways.

- HRM must build networks and shared people communities around the strategic objectives of the business to ensure competitiveness.

- The HRM function will focus externally and internally and look more like operations management, dealing with vendors and managing the supply chain.

| | |
|---|---|
| Rapid Deployment Specialist | • The new goal for HRM will be to manage markets, some of which will be rapidly changing markets. HRM will anticipate what rapidly changing product markets and business strategies will require by way of human capabilities and find ways to deliver it. |
| | • Work assignments are fluid, involving responsibility for results rather than tasks. |
| | • The future resides in the capacity to design a versatile, evolving, flexible HRM architecture that supports an increasing pace of change. The organizational infrastructure needs to be reconfigurable, that is, elements of information, business processes, and organizational design must be capable of being combined in different ways to meet situational needs. |
| | • Common purpose and core values supplant tight managerial control systems and job descriptions. |
| | • Widespread sharing of organizational information is necessary. |

Human capital stewardship prescribes a relationship between the organization and its employees in which the organization leads without dominating and facilitates followers without controlling them. Stewardship allows for a relationship between organizations and employees in which each makes significant, self-responsible contributions to organizational success (Daft, 1999).

Some of the challenges facing the human resource management function as stewards of human capital include the following.

- Intellectual capital is not owned by the employer but is bought and sold in human capital markets. How do you find and obtain that intellectual capital? Do you rent or purchase that intellectual capital?
- Workers are volunteers or free agents. How do you attract, motivate, and retain volunteers? How do you facilitate volunteers' identification with the organization? Nonprofit and volunteer organizations deal with these issues on a daily basis. How can HRM adapt practices from these organizations for knowledge workers in private corporations?
- Market contracts replace (most) employment contracts. Employment contracts are more long-term; market contracts are more short-term and project-based. How do you obtain the needed level of commitment from workers who have market rather than employment contracts?
- Human resource management must ensure that the organization's human capital is available, capable, and effective, and that it grows in value. How do you manage employee flows (into, within, and out of the organization) to ensure the maximum

continuous capability? Some of the best college football teams produce consistently winning teams over time by balancing the mix of experienced and novice players to win both now and in the future. Furthermore, like organizations in the knowledge economy, these football teams constantly worry about key players being attracted to professional status before completing their college careers.

- Human resource management must broker HR services, such as talent acquisition, learning, and so forth. How do you find the HR services that are available and that could help your organization? How do you choose among providers? How do you integrate disparate service providers into a cohesive whole?

- Human resource management must leverage human capital (that is, focus on doing the right things and gaining maximum output for a given input). How do you combine human capital for maximum output? How do you combine human and other capital for maximum output?

- There is a greater dependence on key knowledge workers and ensuring they are attracted and retained. How do you create a work environment that adapts to meet the needs of key workers? How do you sense and respond to the needs of key workers? There will be higher entry-level requirements for employment. How do you challenge and motivate knowledge workers? How do you create opportunities for personal growth among knowledge workers?

- Careers replace jobs. How do you balance the need for corporate as well as professional identification and commitment? How do you create an environment that best utilizes temporary talent as long as you have it? How do you match the needs of the corporation and the needs of temporary talent?
- Policies regarding proprietary information become more challenging to design. What policies should govern non-compete agreements? How is proprietary information defined and distinguished from tacit knowledge that must be shared in a boundaryless organization?

## Knowledge Facilitator

It is not enough to simply hire talented employees and put them to work. For an organization to gain a competitive advantage in the knowledge economy, it must be able to create and disseminate knowledge among its employees and often among its customers, suppliers, and the firms that make complementary products, as well. This knowledge sharing can range from the mundane simple fix of a computer problem shared by an employee via email to the reengineering of a process disseminated throughout all units in the organization via a training program to ensuring that products made by other organizations make full use of a firm's product functionality. As Intel discovered, not only was it essential for its own employees to share technology advances among themselves, it was equally important for firms making the software and hardware that uses their microprocessors to incorporate new concepts into their products. Cutting-edge technology allows employees in the lower levels of organizations to seize opportunities and get breakthrough ideas to the market first. Language barriers are eroding: Employees and freelancers anywhere in the world will soon be able to converse in numerous languages online without the need for translators.

A new role for HRM is to facilitate organizational learning and knowledge sharing between employees, among departments, throughout the organization, and with external co-producers. Some of the challenges facing HRM in this role include the following.

- There is an increased emphasis on learning and encouraging people to learn continuously. How do you find people who want to learn? How do you encourage employees to learn continuously? How do you facilitate continuous learning? How do you retain work-life balance with continuous learning?

- There is a need to manage knowledge and data actively and directly (acquisition, dissemination, and so forth). How can knowledge be acquired and made available to those who need it when they need it? How should knowledge be managed? What types of information systems best meet organizational needs?
- The organization must tap into all employees' knowledge as sources of innovation. How do you identify sources of employee knowledge? How do you elicit that knowledge from employees?
- Human resource management must facilitate the sharing of knowledge acquired by employees. What types of mediators facilitate the sharing of knowledge? How much knowledge sharing should be computer-mediated and how much should be face-to-face?
- Human resource management must determine how to reward knowledge acquisition and sharing. Rewarding knowledge acquisition may be the easier challenge of the two. How do you get employees to share knowledge that, once shared, will no longer provide them with

a personal competitive advantage and will make them expendable?

- Information must be made available and accessible to employees. How much information should be made available to employees? How do you make information available to employees? What information formats facilitate effective communication? How do you both make information widely accessible and still retain proprietary confidentiality?

- New knowledge must lead to new behaviors. As David Garvin (1993) explains, knowledge is of little use unless a firm is able to adjust its actions, decisions, and relationships to capitalize on the insight. What organizational capabilities are crucial for a firm to use knowledge more adeptly, quickly, and creatively? What processes enable rapid learning, unlearning, and relearning? How can employees maintain a consistent focus for their efforts while constantly incorporating new ideas?

## Relationship Builder

Along with facilitating the sharing of knowledge within an organization, another important new HRM role is that of relationship builder. In an increasingly fast-paced and turbulent environment, more emphasis will be placed on the relationships created and sustained among employees within and across organizations. Rather than building assets on their balance sheets, companies will develop partnerships, oftentimes creating intense collaborators out of a company's fiercest rivals.

In the new role of relationship builder, the HRM function will create programs and practices that enable employees to encourage, facilitate, nourish, and sustain relationships among fellow employees, customers, suppliers, firms in complementary arenas, and at times, even rivals. The power of relationships is in creating synergy within the organization and across the marketplace. Agile combinations of employees who have developed relationship networks can create more value for the organization than the mere sum of their individual contributions.

One of the lessons from the work on complex adaptive systems (Pascale, 1999) is that relationships hold the key to organizational resourcefulness and resilience. The ways in which people interact substantially determine the extent to which the full benefits of their capabilities are realized by a firm. Some of the challenges facing HRM in this role include the following.

- There is an increased emphasis on cross-functional teamwork. How do you organize optimal team structures? How do you create a whole that is greater than the sum of its parts? How do you achieve balance between individual (functional) loyalties and team identification? How do you create and dissolve project teams and sustain high performance? There is no single, correct answer. W.L. Gore and Associates rely on what they term a "lattice structure" (Shipper & Manz, 1992) that emphasizes integration, whereas Technical and Computer Graphics (TCG) relies on a cellular form that emphasizes flexible autonomy (Miles et al., 1997).

- Technology will make information more accessible and join people together in different ways. What technologies can link people together? How do you train people to maximize the effectiveness of these technologies? How do you minimize communication failures? What dimensions of social capital are required to translate technology advances into competitive advantage? Human resource management may be able to capitalize on the structural links created by enterprise resource planning (ERP) systems, for example, to enrich other forms of social capital.
- Human resource management must build networks and shared people communities around the strategic objectives of the business

to ensure competitiveness. How do you persuasively communicate the organization's strategic objectives? How do you build commitment to those objectives when much of your workforce has only a partial relationship with the organization? Kaplan and Norton (2001) suggest that HRM can use individual balanced scorecards to effectively communicate strategic themes and to gain commitment across diverse constituencies.

- The HRM function will focus externally and internally and look more like operations management, dealing with vendors and managing the supply chain. How do you gain the trust of other members of the supply chain? What information do you share among members of the supply chain? How do you maximize effectiveness and efficiency in the supply chain?

## Rapid Deployment Specialist

The rapid pace and constantly changing environment that many organizations and industries confront creates another new challenge and new role for HRM: the rapid deployment specialist. Competitive advantage gained by bringing new products to the market before competitors will be short-lived. Technology, and a variety of different ways to create value, will allow competitors to meet or exceed such advantages almost instantaneously. Rather than creating and sustaining a long-term competitive advantage that is defended over time, many organizations in the knowledge economy will instead opt for short-term, in-and-out, guerrilla-like tactics, which allow them to take advantage of fleeting opportunities in the marketplace. Once the advantage has been achieved, these organizations will move on to the next opportunity. Many whole companies will be intentionally ephemeral, formed to create new technologies or products only to be absorbed by sponsor companies when their missions are accomplished. Other firms will design their strategies around maneuverability to reflect their turbulent and unpredictable marketplaces.

Consequently, the HRM function will be required to rapidly assemble, concentrate, and deploy specific configurations of human capital to achieve mission-specific strategic goals. Organizations will use various combinations of HRM approaches (such as training, exporting work offshore, and looking for ways to "de-skill" certain jobs) while enriching others to accomplish these objectives. Fortunately, improved information technologies are available, or are being developed, to facilitate this. However, the challenge for HRM in the knowledge economy is substantial and significantly different from HRM in the twentieth century. Some of the challenges facing HR in this role include the following.

- The new goal for HRM will be to manage the contributions individuals make to specific external markets, some of which will be rapidly changing markets. Increasingly, HRM will need to emphasize and understand events taking place beyond the borders of the firm. Human resource management will anticipate what rapidly changing product markets and business strategies will require by way of human capabilities and find ways to deliver it. How can you anticipate what human capabilities may be needed to enact business strategies? How can you prepare human capabilities when markets change rapidly? What mix of core and contingent workers provides maximum flexibility and maximum effectiveness?

- Work assignments are fluid, involving responsibility for results rather than tasks. How do you define what people will do in their work assignments? How do you coordinate across work assignments that are fluid? How do you manage careers when work assignments are fluid? How do you design effective performance measurement systems when the objectives are evolving?

- The future resides in the capacity to design a versatile, evolving, flexible HRM architecture that not only supports but also sets the agenda for an increasing pace of change. The organizational infrastructure needs to be reconfigurable, that is, elements of information, business processes, and organizational design must be capable of being combined in different ways to meet situational needs. What types of information are needed for rapid deployment? How do you utilize employees as intact teams that are redeployed, as project workers working on several projects simultaneously, and as components in a self-organizing system?

- Common purpose and core values supplant tight managerial control systems and job descriptions. How do you ensure that needed work gets done? How do you coordinate across jobs and between organizational functions? How do you achieve order without chaos?

- Widespread sharing of organizational information is necessary. How do you share information widely? Who gets access to what information? How do you prevent disclosure of proprietary information?

# Conclusion

One thing is certain: "Our profession, the HRM profession, is at the epicenter of a profound transformation. We have never been so visible—or so vulnerable" (Sartain, 2001). Much like the proverbial dog that chases cars, we may ask, what do we do once we've caught the car? Human resource management can either fail to take advantage of the opportunity and become less important, while other groups assimilate these new roles, or it can carve out a new territory by assuming these new roles, ones that can lead to both greater prominence and greater impact. The next four chapters define each of the four roles and demonstrate how HRM can change to meet the needs of organizations in the knowledge economy.

# Chapter 3

# Human Capital Steward

"An investment in knowledge always pays the
best interest."
—Benjamin Franklin

"Forget land, buildings, or machines—the real
source of wealth today is intelligence, applied
intelligence. We talk glibly of "intellectual
property" without taking on board what it really
means. It isn't just patent rights and brand names;
it is the brains of the place."
—Charles Handy

## What Is Human Capital?

Effective adoption of the human capital
steward role requires appreciation of two issues.
First, there must be a clear understanding of
what is meant by **human capital.** Second, a
compelling rationale must be provided for a
stewardship perspective. In this chapter, we hope
to accomplish both of these purposes. We begin
with a discussion of human capital.

While there is no single accepted definition
of human capital, most authors focus on similar

factors: The collective knowledge, skills, abilities, and other characteristics (that is, all of the capabilities combined) of an organization's employees and managers that create a capacity (potential that can be realized) for competitive advantage. Human capital is created by changes in people that develop skills and capabilities enabling them to act in new ways (Coleman, 1988). Here are some of the definitions of human capital to illustrate the range of conceptualizations.

- Human capital is "the knowledge, skills, and capabilities of individuals that have economic value to an organization" (Bohlander, Snell, & Sherman, 2001).

- Human capital is "the collective value of an organization's know-how. Human capital refers to the value, usually not reflected in accounting systems, which results from the investment an organization must make to recreate the knowledge in its employees" (Cortada & Woods, 1999).

- Human capital is "all individual capabilities, the knowledge, skill, and experience of the company's employees and managers" (Edvinsson & Malone, 1997).

- Human capital is "capabilities, knowledge, skills, and experience, all of them embodied in and inseparable from the individual" (Dess & Pickens, 1999).

- "Human capital comprises all the intangible assets that people bring to their jobs. It's the currency of work, the specie that workers trade for financial and other rewards." It consists of knowledge (command of a body of facts); skill (facility, developed through practice, with the means of carrying out a task); talent (inborn facility for performing a task); and behavior (observable ways of acting that contribute to accomplishing a task (Davenport, 1999).

Human capital can be broken down into several components. The analysis of human capital proposed by Dess and Pickens (1999) is one of the more comprehensive models. They see human capital as comprising the following elements.

- **Motor Skills:** The ability to grasp, place, move, and manipulate objects in coordinated movements
- **Information Gathering (Perception) Skills:** Sensory, perceptual, and interpretative capabilities
- **Information-Processing (Cognitive) Skills:** The ability to reason, analyze, and make decisions
- **Communication Skills:** The ability to listen, communicate, and share information and ideas
- **Experience:** Know-how (and perspective) from having done the task before

- **Knowledge:** Knowledge of self, the job, the organization, and the environment
- **Social Skills:** The ability to interface, coordinate, and collaborate productively with others
- **Values, Beliefs, and Attitudes:** Personal values that shape perceptions, performance, and attitudes

Human capital is similar to, but different from, the traditional (job-based) view of KSAOs (knowledge, skills, abilities, and other characteristics). The KSAOs are defined as follows (Spector, 1997). **Knowledge** is what a person knows that is relevant to the job. **Skill** is what a person is able to do on the job. **Ability** (mental, physical, and psychomotor) is the capacity to learn a skill. **Other personal characteristics** include attitudes, beliefs, personality characteristics, temperaments, and values. As can be seen, human capital is a more expansive and integrative concept.

In the traditional view of KSAOs, only those elements of human capital that are directly related to task performance on specific jobs are included. This restricted perspective came about largely because of legal regulations. The Americans with Disabilities Act, for example, requires employers to focus on only those KSAOs that are directly job-related "essential tasks." In the human capital view, however, all of the various talents, attributes, capabilities, and insights a person brings to the workplace are included (*non – job-related and directly job-related*). Thus, an employee's music skills may not be typically considered as directly relevant to effective job performance for many jobs. Musical talent may play a significant role in an individual's value-creating potential, however, when considered in conjunction with the other KSAOs the employee brings to the workplace. Developing musical skills, for example, may allow an employee to design more creative solutions to a problem, or may develop a habit of disciplined rehearsal, or may form the basis for relationships with other employees that facilitate the building of social capital. Nontraditional capabilities may enhance job performance in indirect, but quite valuable, ways.

Human capital, along with structural capital and relationship capital (see definitions in Chapter 1), constitute the **strategic capability** of an organization, a readiness for the present and an ability to adapt in the future. As an illustration, consider a London cabby (Curry & Cavendish, 1998). Since most cabbies are self-employed, their "companies" consist of their personal financial capital, their customers (relationship capital), their cab (structural capital), and themselves (the human capital). The cab on its own does not generate wealth, but the cab used by the knowledgeable cabby is a productive organization of one. As the cabby develops a loyal clientele based perhaps on his reliability, skilled driving, knowledge of traffic patterns in the city, and pleasing personality, the integration of human capital, structural capital, and relationship capital creates a source of sustainable competitive advantage. Thus, customers, cab, and cabbie combine to represent a strategic capability that has both immediate benefits and long-term potential.

Some human capital is valuable across all settings. That is, some human capital acquired and used by one employer (that is, a general skill) is equally valuable across all other employers. For example, the ability to read is valuable in (almost) all work settings. Consequently, it is a general skill. In the earliest formulations of human capital theory (for instance, Becker, 1964), theorists predicted that employers would not invest their training budgets in "general training" (for instance, training employees to read), since this would make employees more valuable to other employers. Thus, if an organization invested in employees' problem-solving abilities and those employees left to work for other employers after acquiring those skills, the organization would have essentially "trained the competitors' employees."

**General skills** are acquired through public education and self-initiative, at least according to the theory. However, during the economic boom of the 1990s, employers frequently found that many in the workforce did not have the general skills needed to perform adequately on the job.

Thus, many employers started providing general training, contrary to the predictions of the theory, to compensate for skill deficiencies in a tight labor market. Employer-supported education, such as subsidizing employees in their pursuit of undergraduate degrees regardless of the direct relevance of their majors to their current jobs, is an extension of this expanded orientation. Often this type of general skill development is used to attract employees with desirable attitudes toward continuous learning and self-improvement.

In the new view of human capital, training in non – job-related areas may be as important as job-specific training, since it expands the knowledge repertoires of individuals and thus extends the knowledge repertoires of organizations. Through his interviews with stunt people in Hollywood, Wiener (1996) demonstrates how broad skill repertoires can be invaluable in a job or to an organization. Stunt people typically have diverse and unusual backgrounds, from crop dusting to rodeo riding, that prepare them for virtually any kind of stunt, from falling off a building to being run over by a car. With a larger repertoire of human capital, organizations may resemble stunt people and may have greater strategic capability enabling them to deal effectively with almost any emerging situation.

The value of some human capital is context-specific (Lengnick-Hall & Lengnick-Hall, 1988). Some human capital is valuable only to a specific organization (**firm-specific skills**). For example, knowing a firm's filing system is firm-specific. It has value only to a specific firm and is of little use if the employee joins a new organization. Some human capital is valuable only within the context of a specific industry **(industry-specific skills)**. For example, technical jargon is often industry-specific. It has value only within a specific industry. An individual who changes from a marketing job in the furniture industry to a marketing job in the video game industry will likely need to learn a whole new language. To the extent that employees' skills are specific to an organization or a particular setting, their mobility and transferability are reduced, their value to the firm is enhanced, and their replacement costs are increased. Thus, early conceptualizations of human capital theory (for instance, Becker, 1964) predicted that organizations would only invest in firm-specific training, since it would enhance the value of the employees only to the specific organization and not make them more valuable to other employers.

Some authors and researchers have proposed that the strategic importance of human capital is determined by two main factors: uniqueness or replaceability, and value (Stewart, 1997; Lepak & Snell, 1999; Burton-Jones, 1999). **Uniqueness** refers to the degree of context-specificity of the human capital or the degree to which it cannot be transferred to other organizations. For human capital to be considered unique, it must be relatively rare and difficult to imitate or replace. Barney (1995) explains that history and timing, path dependence, requirements for complementary assets, social complexity, causal ambiguity, and continuous investment contribute to making imitation more difficult. Uniqueness is closely linked to the sustainability of the competitive advantage resulting from the application of human capital.

**Value** refers to the degree to which the human capital lowers costs or provides increased service or product features that matter to customers. Value reflects the significance and durability of the need that is being filled by the application of human capital. Just because individuals are very good at doing something does not mean that their human capital is valuable. Extensive experience in conventional steel-making technology was a competitive liability rather than a value-creating capability, when thin-slab, continuous-casting, and mini-mill technologies redefined the industry, because the existing expertise made it less likely that the new, more efficient technologies would be embraced. Time-tested expertise in the established technologies made it more difficult for individuals to recognize the benefits of new and unfamiliar innovations.

Value is closely linked to the competitive contribution of human capital. Human capital with a wide variety of potential applications is likely to be more valuable over the long term than extremely specialized capabilities. A good bedside manner, therefore, may be more valuable for most physicians than extensive experience in treating patients who have been bitten by a brown recluse spider. However, deep, specialized knowledge may be required to respond effectively to particular situational needs. Scientists who have extensive knowledge of hazardous materials may be especially valuable when an explosion takes place at a chemical plant.

Different combinations of uniqueness and value yield human capital that has more or less strategic importance.

- **High Uniqueness/High Value** reflects human capital that is very important to the organization. It is firm-specific and directly linked to the organization's strategy. Examples include research scientists, computer scientists, and product developers in biotechnology firms, since these individuals provide the competence-enhancing foundation for the firm's work.

- **High Uniqueness/Low Value** reflects human capital that is necessary for doing business (and is specialized and not readily available to all firms) but tangentially linked to strategy. It is firm-specific but not directly linked to the organization's strategy. Examples include attorneys, consultants, and data-processing specialists in automobile manufacturers. These individuals provide the expertise necessary to accomplish basic business requirements, but they do not offer a potential source of competitive advantage, since they do not contribute directly to customer value.

- **Low Uniqueness/High Value** reflects human capital that is low on firm-specificity but directly linked to the organization's strategy. Examples include salespeople in retail stores and truck drivers for United Parcel Service (UPS). The competitive value from these types of human capital flows from the style, quality, and exceptional performance of individuals rather than from the basic nature of the work that is performed.

- **Low Uniqueness/Low Value** reflects human capital that is low on firm-specificity and not directly linked to the organization's strategy. Examples include clerical workers, maintenance employees, and receptionists. This type of human capital is necessary but does not rely on specialized, path-dependent skill investments and is not a potential source of competitive advantage for the organization.

Human capital is difficult but not impossible to measure. Accountants are reluctant to report financial valuations of human capital. This is the case despite the fact that many of the supposedly "hard numbers" that accountants use require subjective judgments (for example, depreciation). Accounting does allow some intangibles to be included in the balance sheet, however, if there has been a transaction involved (such as research and development expenses; costs for concessions, patents, and licenses; and paid goodwill). This conventional accounting limitation is one of the arguments made by Kaplan and Norton (2001) for the use of a more comprehensive and balanced assessment of organizations. In their balanced scorecard, for example, firms establish explicit goals and measures for human capital development in the "innovation and learning" segment of the strategy map.

Some companies have made major efforts to develop metrics useful for characterizing their human capital. Skandia, an international financial services company, is a pioneer in measuring and managing human capital. They have developed several useful indexes. Skandia's human capital measures are presented in Table 3.1 (from Edvinsson & Malone, 1997).

Some countries, too, have taken the initiative to assess aspects of their national human capital. Canada is noteworthy in this regard. Statistics Canada has designed an instrument called the Workplace and Employee Survey (WES). This survey collects data on workforce characteristics and job organization, compensation, training, HR functions, establishment performance, business strategy, innovation, and use of government programs. Additionally, the survey collects data from a sample of employees at each establishment and data on job characteristics, education and training, personal and family support programs, compensation, work history, and turnover. Such information can help shape public policy in a way that enhances human capital development and application for national advantage.

In summary, human capital is the collective knowledge, skills, abilities, and other characteristics (that is, all of the capabilities combined) of an organization's employees and managers that create a capacity (potential that can be realized) for competitive advantage. Some human capital is valuable across all work settings, whereas other human capital is valuable only within a specific organization or industry context. Human capital is strategically important to a specific organization if it is unique, valuable, and difficult to replicate. And, while human capital is difficult to measure, the task is not impossible. In an interview with Brook Manville (Manville, 2002), Gary S. Becker, Nobel Laureate in economics, argued that the best companies in the knowledge economy will likely set up human capital accounting systems, so they can track and assess their return on human capital investment. He predicted such firms publicly reporting what they spend and invest in this area.

Table 3.1 Skandia's Measures of Human Capital

| Measure | Interpretation |
| --- | --- |
| Number of full-time employees | Indicates the size of the core group of workers |

| | |
|---|---|
| Full-time permanent employees as percentage of total employment | Indicates the proportion of core- to non-core workers: Too small, and the organization may not be able to perpetuate itself; too large, and the organization may carry too much labor overhead |
| Average age of full-time permanent employees | Older, may have more experience that is valuable in some industries; younger, may have more current knowledge that is valuable in some industries |
| Average years with company of full-time permanent employees | Longer, may be more resistant to change; shorter, may be more receptive |
| Annual turnover of full-time permanent employees | Higher turnover may indicate more loss of valued organizational memory |
| Per capita annual cost of training, communication, and support programs for full-time permanent employees | Indicates the organization's commitment to maintaining the core group of workers |
| Full-time permanent employees who spend less than 50% of work hours at a corporate facility (also, percentage of total workforce; percentage of full-time permanent employees; per capita annual cost of training, communications, and support programs) | May indicate the organization's HRM flexibility; may indicate employees "closeness" to customers |
| Number of full-time temporary employees (also, percentage of total workforce; average years with company of full-time temporary employees) | May indicate the organization's HRM flexibility |

| | |
|---|---|
| Per capita annual cost of training and support programs for full-time temporary employees | Indicates organization's commitment to all of its employees |
| Number of part-time employees and full-time contractors (also, percentage of the total workforce; average duration of contract) | May indicate the organization's HRM flexibility |
| Percentage of company managers with advanced business degrees (also, advanced science and engineering degrees; advanced liberal arts degrees) | Indicates breadth of knowledge among management |
| Percentage of company managers of different nationality than the company registry | Indicates global diversity repertoire of management |
| Company managers assigned to full-time permanent employees | Indicates commitment of management time to various groups; or indicates self-management |

From Edvinsson, L. & Malone, M.S. (1997). Intellectual capital: Realizing Your Company's True Value By Finding Its Hidden Roots. New York: HarperBusiness.

# Human Capital Steward: A New Role for Human Resource Management

Stewardship metaphors are commonly used with natural resources, such as land, fish, and forests. These metaphors focus on preserving, conserving, sustaining, growing, and developing the natural resources. Furthermore, these metaphors focus on the future and on ensuring that the resources will be available and on thriving beyond the current time horizon. Peter Block (1993) defines stewardship in an organization context as follows:

> Stewardship is to hold something in trust for another. Historically, stewardship was a means to protect a kingdom while those rightfully in charge were away, or more often, to govern for the sake of an underage king. Stewardship is defined ... as the willingness to be accountable for the well being of the larger organization by operating in service, rather than in control of those around us. Stated simply, it is accountability without control or compliance.

Stewardship is a pivotal shift in HRM thinking. It is about being deeply accountable to others as well as to the organization, without trying to control, define meaning and purpose, or take care of them (Daft, 1999). It is about guiding the organization without dominating it and facilitating employees without controlling them. "Stewardship allows for a relationship between leaders and followers in which each makes significant, self-responsible contributions to organizational success. In addition, it gives followers a chance to use their minds, bodies, and spirits on the job, thereby allowing them to be more 'complete' human beings" (Daft, 1999). The focus of stewardship is on the people actually doing the work, making products, providing services, or interacting directly with customers. The following principles provide a framework for HR stewardship (Daft, 1999; Block, 1993).

1.  *Reorient toward a partnership assumption.* A reorientation of this nature means moving away from the paternalistic, policing role HRM has had in the past, that is, "Here are the rules; ask our permission; if you don't do what we say, we'll punish you." It reflects an understanding that partners have a right, and even at times an obligation, to say "no" to each other. Partners are honest with each other. They don't hide information from each other, and they don't protect each other from bad news. This reorientation for HRM acts on the belief that partners are jointly responsible for outcomes and for defining vision and purpose. To move toward a partnership orientation, HRM needs to unlearn habits focused on imposing regulations or on waiting for direction from corporate leadership.

2.  *Localize decisions and power to those closest to the work and the customer.* Disintermediation—or eliminating the middleman, in this case, managers—is fundamental to an HR stewardship perspective. People are not hired to simply

plan and manage the work of others; everyone does some of the core work some of the time. Likewise, everyone is responsible for thinking strategically, being on the alert for opportunities, providing early warning of problems, and responding to situational needs. This also means that HRM should encourage employees to take ownership and responsibility for their own human capital development and should not assume a paternalistic "we'll worry about that for you" attitude.

3. *Recognize and reward the value of workers.* Rewards are linked to the success of the whole organization. Workers earn their rewards by delivering real value to customers. Non–value-added activities are eliminated, even if they are something the firm has learned to do especially well or particularly efficiently. The focus is on work that contributes to meeting real needs both inside the firm and for customers. Rewards are based on contribution rather than on hierarchy. This means that HRM needs to thoroughly understand how their firm intends to create competitive value and to be able to design ways to create the needed human capital in anticipation of strategic initiatives.

4. *Expect core work teams to build the organization.* Teams define goals, maintain controls, and create a nurturing environment. Teams are expected to choose how they respond to changes in the marketplace or the work context. Teams design selection, compensation, appraisal, and training practices and are held accountable for the outcomes that result from these processes. Human resource management's responsibilities are more in the realm of mentor and teacher than supervisor. It sets the parameters to ensure consistency and provides its expertise through education to expand the firm's competence. HRM must see its "primary contribution as creating a governance system of partnership and self-management" (Block, 1993).

5. *Support the core workers by procuring needed talent from a variety of sources when it is needed, where it is needed, and only for as long as it is needed.* From a stewardship perspective, HRM serves as a facilitator, a resource for gathering and distributing human capital, and an origin of advice and expertise when unfamiliar issues arise. The goal of HR stewardship is not to create mutual dependence but to create individuals

throughout the firm who are resourceful and able to take on challenges, confident that the necessary infrastructure, people, and tangible resources will be available when they are needed.

To fulfill the expectations of the human capital steward role, HRM needs to focus on three major factors: (1) investments, (2) flexibility, and (3) leveraging. Human resource management must be the primary source of information on how, when, and where to make human capital investments in the same way that the finance group in an organization is the primary source of information on how to make financial investments. Human resource management must be the leader in developing individual and organizational flexibility so human capital can be used to its maximum competitive advantage. It must provide a broad perspective on how to combine and integrate the human capital of the organization to achieve the maximum productivity from the resources and to create synergy for the firm. Each of these factors will be discussed next.

# Human Capital Investments

Investments in human capital involve both financial and commitment components. Financially, human capital investments include direct costs associated with pay and benefits as well as indirect costs, such as training and education. Commitment entails both duration of the employment relationship and the psychological contract between the employee and the organization.

As a human capital steward, one role for HRM is to ensure that sound human capital investments are made by the organization. Ulrich (1998) describes five different human capital investment choices designed to create both competence and commitment to the firm:

- **Buy:** Acquire new talent by hiring individuals from outside the firm or from elsewhere within the firm.
- **Build:** Train or develop talent through formal job training, job rotation, job assignment, and action learning.
- **Borrow:** Form partnerships with people outside the firm (for example, consultants, vendors, customers, or suppliers) to find new ideas.
- **Bounce:** Remove individuals with low or sub-par performance.
- **Bind:** Retain the most talented employees.

As noted earlier, the more unique (firm-specific) and more valuable (directly related to competitive strategy) the human capital that a particular worker possesses, the greater the investment that should be made in that individual. In the knowledge economy, human capital can be obtained from either inside or outside of the organization more easily than ever before. Greater financial and commitment investments are typically made to human capital within the organization. For human capital acquired from outside the organization, financial investments may (in some cases) be similar to those acquired internally; however commitment investments for external workers range from little to none.

There are three sources of human capital within the organization that receive the greatest financial and commitment investments: the core group, the associate group, and the peripheral group (Burton-Jones, 1999) (see Table 3.2).

The **core group** is comprised of those workers who have unique and valuable human capital. They are responsible for high-level knowledge integration functions and for planning, coordinating, and controlling the organization's activities. This group is roughly equivalent to what Stewart (1997) describes as "strategists," although it is important to note that many of these individuals may not be located at the top of the conventional organizational hierarchy.

The **associate group** is those workers who have firm-specific knowledge that is typically focused more in their areas of specialization. They are responsible for controlling the main operational functions of the firm, such as finance, marketing, and production, or the core processes, such as product development or order fulfillment.

This group is equivalent to what Stewart (1997) describes as "talent."

Table 3.2 Human Capital Investments

| Human Capital Source | Definition | Level of Investment |
|---|---|---|
| Core Group | Those workers who have unique and valuable human capital; responsible for high-level knowledge integration functions and for planning, coordinating, and controlling the organization's activities | High |
| Associate Group | Those workers who have firm-specific knowledge that is typically focused more in their areas of specialization; responsible for controlling the main operational functions of the firm, such as finance, marketing, and production | High |
| Peripheral Group | Those workers who have high levels of firm-specific knowledge of the firm's day-to-day operations; boundary-spanners, responsible for managing the interface with external suppliers and customers | High |
| Flexhire Workers | Those workers who support the peripheral group in their responsibilities of administration, maintenance, and other similar functions; those who have less unique and less valuable human capital; three types—temporary workers, part-time workers, and work sharing | Low |

| Mediated Services | Those workers who support the peripheral group in their responsibilities of administration, maintenance, and other similar functions; less firm-specific knowledge is necessary, the services of workers can be delivered to the firm, with the assistance of, or directly by, an independent intermediary agency; two types—staffing services and outsourcing services | Low |
|---|---|---|
| Dependent Contractors | Those with a medium-to-high level of firm-specific knowledge and whose value to the organization is high; the work they do is either not directly related to the organization's strategy, or they are used because the organization wants to maintain financial flexibility for growth | Medium |
| Independent Contractors | Those with a low level of firm-specific knowledge, but their value to the organization is high; the work they do is either not directly related to the organization's strategy, or they are used because the organization wants to maintain financial flexibility for growth | Medium |

The **peripheral group** encompasses those workers who have high levels of firm-specific knowledge of the organization's day-to-day operations. They are boundary-spanners, responsible for managing the interface with external suppliers and customers. This group is equivalent to what Stewart (1997) describes as "resource providers."

There are four sources of human capital outside of the organization: flexhires, mediated services, dependent contractors, and independent contractors. Although some financial investments to these workers may be similar to those within the organization, commitment levels are much lower.

**Flexhire workers** are those who have less unique and less valuable human capital. Some firm-specific knowledge is required, however, which is why these workers are not obtained from staffing services. They primarily support the peripheral group in their responsibilities of administration, maintenance, and other similar functions. Their human capital is needed on an occasional basis, so organizational commitments to them are low.

Three types of flexhires are: temporary workers, part-time workers, and work-sharing arrangements. Temporary workers typically are employed full-time (complete workdays) but for a specific short term. Part-time workers typically are employed for a longer duration but with fewer hours of work per day. Work-sharing is an arrangement whereby two part-time employees share one full-time regular assignment.

**Mediated services,** like flexhire sources, support the peripheral group. Workers from this source have less unique and less valuable human capital. Since less firm-specific knowledge is necessary, the services of workers can be delivered to the firm with the assistance of, or directly by, an independent intermediary agency. Organizations make virtually no commitments to these workers.

There are two primary types of mediated services: staffing and outsourcing. Staffing services (for instance, Snelling and Snelling) are organizations that recruit, often train, and supply workers to organizations. Outsourcing services (for instance, benefits administered by a third party) are organizations that directly replace functions that would otherwise be carried out within the organization.

**Dependent contractors** are those with a medium-to-high level of firm-specific knowledge and those whose value to the organization is high. Dependent contractors typically rely on one or a few firms for the majority of their business. Aircraft manufacturers, such as Boeing, use dependent contractors from many of their suppliers to complete specialized tasks, such as preparing engines for installation. Organizations make low-level commitments to these workers. Commitments are usually contingent on how well the organization performs financially. The human capital of dependent contractors is of a type that organizations typically do not want to internalize, because it is either not directly related to the organization's strategy, or because the organization wants to maintain financial flexibility for growth.

**Independent contractors** are those with a low level of firm-specific knowledge but those whose value to the organization is high. Independent contractors are typically not dependent on any one firm for their business. The human capital of independent contractors typically supports technical, professional, and specialty services. Organizations make virtually no commitments to these workers.

To sum up, as a human capital steward, HRM must aid organizations in making wise investments of limited resources. Human resource professionals must use their expertise regarding trade-offs among the various sources of human capital to achieve the best results for the firm both long term and short term. In addition, HRM must create a work context that truly capitalizes on the human capital investments it recommends. For example, if an organization relies on a large proportion of flexhire workers, the firm must make it easy for these employees to quickly learn the ropes and blend into organizational processes. Likewise, HRM must make it efficient and attractive for those in the associate group to both use and share their specialized expertise in ways that enhance the firm's long-term knowledge repertoire.

As indicated, organizational investments in human capital can be either financial, commitment-related, or both. The more unique and valuable the human capital, the greater should be both the financial and commitment investments. Some human capital obtained externally may receive larger financial investments but lower commitment investments than that found within organizations. However, this transactional approach presumes that the need for the externally purchased knowledge or skills is fairly transitory. Maintaining a proper balance among the various sources of human capital is crucial for ensuring that an organization is able to stay competitive and create strategic capability.

# Human Capital Flexibility

Human capital flexibility is both a process and an outcome. By *process*, we mean that human capital flexibility refers to an organization's ability to sense and respond quickly to changing strategic and environmental needs. By *outcome*, we mean that human capital flexibility reflects both diversity across the totality of human capital available to a firm and an ability to capitalize on the right capabilities for a particular situation. That is, *flexibility* refers to the depth and breadth of the human capabilities and to the organization's human capital readiness for meeting multiple challenges.

As a human capital steward, one role of HRM is to create human capital flexibility. Human capital flexibility enhances organizational effectiveness and survival. Human capital flexibility can be created in two primary ways (Wright & Snell, 1998): (1) developing a human capital pool with a broad array of skills, and (2) developing HR systems that can be adapted quickly (see Table 3.3).

**Resource flexibility** refers to the number of potential alternative uses to which human capital can be applied. For example, an employee who is an adept problem solver has a more flexible skill than an employee who is an expert in using a specific piece of sophisticated machinery. There are two quite different approaches to achieving resource flexibility among a firm's employees. One way is to maintain a smaller (in size) workforce but one that has a wide range of capabilities embedded in the human capital. In this case, the same human capital can be used to meet the needs of a variety of situations. Kinko's, the nationwide business service operation, relies on this approach to meet the broad array of business service needs their copy centers provide. Cross-training and job rotation are two traditional HR practices that can facilitate this approach to resource flexibility. Similarly, Southwest Airlines relies on its highly committed and effectively cross-trained employees to do whatever is needed, regardless of whether their primary role is pilot, flight crew, or baggage handler, to ensure a 15-minute turnaround time.

Table 3.3 Human Capital Flexibility

| Type of Flexibility | Definition | Strategies |
| --- | --- | --- |
| Resource | The number of potential alternative uses to which employee skills can be applied | • Maintain a smaller (in size) workforce but one that has a broad array of human capital—the same human capital can be used to meet the needs of a variety of situations; cross-training and job rotation are two traditional HR practices that can facilitate this approach to resource flexibility<br><br>• Have a larger (in size) workforce consisting of individuals with more narrowly defined and different human capital—different configurations of human capital can be assembled, deployed, and reassembled for each different situation |
| Coordination | The extent to which HR practices can be adapted and applied across a variety of situations | • Make HR practices more generalizable across jobs, departments, and soon.<br><br>• Decentralize HRM and provide only general parameters |

A second way to achieve resource flexibility is to have a larger (in size) workforce consisting of individuals with more narrowly defined—and different—human capital. With this approach, different configurations of human capital can be assembled, deployed, and reassembled for each different situation. Building contractors that orchestrate the work of electricians, carpenters, decorators, painters, plumbers, and a variety of other specialists to reflect the needs of each different job typically rely on this second approach. Team-based work structures with specialists facilitate this form of resource flexibility. The approaches are not mutually exclusive. As a case in point, Army Special Forces teams combine both approaches to resource flexibility: small, team-based work structures; each individual has some specific skill set; and deliberate redundancy in skills across team members to enable the team to deal with unexpected contingencies.

**Coordination flexibility** refers to the extent to which HR practices can be adapted and applied across a variety of situations. The more generally applicable a HR practice is across jobs and situations, the more easily it can be adapted to a particular situation. For example, management by objectives is a performance appraisal technique that can be quickly tailored to a job or situation, whereas a behaviorally anchored rating system (BARS) generally reflects a particular job in a particular setting and therefore is more limited in its application potential across organizations. With the increasing use of multiple sources of human capital, as described previously, organizations will need to either develop more generalizable (that is, generally applicable) centralized HR practices or allow more decentralized HR practices that meet specific situational conditions but operate within general organizational parameters. Furthermore, with the increasing pace of change in some markets and the need to marshal and concentrate human capital quickly, organizations will have to reduce, or in some cases eliminate, long HR practice implementation periods. Maintaining a small core group of workers, supplemented by human capital obtained externally for specific temporal needs, may be the only way to remain competitive in the future.

Flexibility over time refers to the extent to which HRM has created a learning organization and developed individuals who expect to grow and change on their jobs. With the rapid pace of technology change and the premium placed on organizational agility, it is unreasonable for employees to expect that the knowledge, skills, abilities, and other behaviors they have when they enter a firm will be sufficient to enable them to contribute to firm performance over a long period of time. Human capital flexibility, then, is not just the range of employee talents and ease of application to a variety of purposes, it is also the ability to augment those talents as new needs arise and to unlearn behaviors and perspectives that are no longer useful or appropriate.

In summary, as a human capital steward, HRM must aid organizations in creating flexibility. With rapidly changing environments and an increased pace of doing business, organizations must be flexible, adaptable, and adjustable to survive and to thrive. Human capital flexibility entails having the right mix of human capital available when needed. Human capital flexibility entails being able to adapt human capital to fit diverse needs in diverse situations. Human capital flexibility means that firms can change their repertoire as situations change. Maintaining human capital flexibility is an important factor in creating organizational flexibility and strategic capability.

# Human Capital Leveraging

Leveraging human capital concerns getting the maximum productivity in terms of targeted results. That is, it involves using human capital effectively (focused on doing the right things) and efficiently (getting maximum output for a given input). Dess and Pickens (1999) describe five ways to achieve human capital leverage based on Hamel and Prahalad's (1993) work:

- Leveraging can be achieved by concentrating resources more effectively on key strategic goals. For example, truck drivers in Mobil's lubricants division volunteered to conduct market surveys at truck stops to provide feedback to people in product development because they understood the relationship between an effective product mix and financial performance (Kaplan & Norton, 2001).

- Leveraging can be achieved by accumulating resources more efficiently. Encouraging technologically sophisticated users to beta test new software before it is broadly offered on the market augments a firm's own technical HR.
- Leveraging can be achieved by complementing resources of one type with those of another to create higher-order value. W.L. Gore and Associates encourages employees to take some of their patented polytetrafluoroethylene (PTFE) material to "play around with," and this open approach has resulted in a variety of creative applications from outerwear to artery replacement to cables used in space.
- Leveraging can be achieved by conserving resources wherever possible. Making it easy for customers to become quasi employees by providing their own service at gas stations increases productivity and efficiency. Providing online trouble-shooting guides for software users reduces the need to maintain costly service personnel.
- Leveraging can be achieved by rapidly recovering resources, minimizing the time between expenditure and payback. Creating conditions that enable employees to quickly transfer what they have learned in a training

session to the job decreases the cycle time for payback from the investment.

Since individuals can work in teams and create synergy—the whole is greater than the sum of its parts—leveraging human capital must be viewed at both the individual and organizational levels (see Table 3.4).

**Concentrating human capital** refers to directing individual and group efforts toward specific goals and outcomes. At the individual level, concentration can be achieved by setting performance targets; designing tasks, incentives and controls to focus efforts on firm priorities; and shaping employee values and attitudes in ways that enhance motivation and performance. One of the most important contributions HRM can make to concentrating individual human capital is improving goal clarity and gaining agreement on the firm's strategic intent. Concentrating human capital at the organizational level can be achieved by: building consensus around strategic goals; using incentive and control systems to focus collective efforts on organizational priorities; and designing organization structures to concentrate resources on the highest-priority activities. To achieve effective organizational concentration, HRM can design processes that ensure consistency of purpose and develop mechanisms to manage conflict constructively.

Table 3.4 Human Capital Leveraging

| Leveraging Factor | Definition | Individual Level | Organizational Level |
|---|---|---|---|
| Concentrating | Providing a strategic focal point for the efforts of individuals, units, and the entire organization | • Setting performance targets | • Building consensus on strategic goals |
| | | • Designing tasks, incentives, and controls to focus efforts on firm priorities | • Using incentive and control systems to focus collective efforts on organizational priorities |
| | | • Shaping employee values and attitudes in ways that enhance motivation and performance | • Designing organization structures to concentrate resources on the highest-priority activities |
| Accumulating | Expanding and extending a firm's reservoir of experience and expertise | • Using well-designed selection and placement practices | • Sharing knowledge, experience, and know-how with customers, suppliers, and business partners |

| Comple- menting | Blending and balancing resources that enhance their mutual value | • Designing tasks and projects to make the best use of individual capabilities | • Designing organizational structures and processes, communications infrastructures, and support systems that integrate individual tasks into efficient, flexible, and responsive organizational processes |
|---|---|---|---|
| | | • Matching employees capabilities to the requirements of the tasks and projects | • Combining individual and organization skills in new ways to create higher-order organizational capabilities |
| | | • Using technology to multiply and enhance individual capabilities | • Using organizational mechanisms and communications technology to improve internal coordination and collaboration |
| | | | • Multiplying the capabilities of the organization with advanced processes, systems, and technology |

| Enhancing | Augmenting resources by investing in their further development and broad application | • Encouraging and facilitating individual learning and providing opportunities for training, skill development, and practice | • Encouraging and facilitating organizational learning and the widespread sharing of knowledge and market intelligence |
|---|---|---|---|
| Conserving | Recycling, co-opting, and shield resources so that their value is leveraged to achieve economies of scope | • Implementing well-designed safety and retention programs | • Implementing standard processes and routines, accomplishing the same results with less labor |
| Recovering | Expediting the rate at which benefits are experienced | • Minimizing the lag between hiring and full productivity | • Minimizing the lag between implementing new technologies (for example, ERP systems) and efficiencies realized from that technology |

Adapted from Dess & Pickens, 1999; Hamel & Prahalad, 1993

**Accumulating human capital** refers to creating a sufficient quantity of the right kinds of human capital to meet organizational needs. At the individual level, this can be achieved by using well-designed selection and placement practices. Accumulating human capital at the organizational level can be achieved by sharing knowledge, experience, and know-how with customers, suppliers, and business partners. As discussed in earlier chapters, HRM can contribute to accumulation by managing human capital that is available beyond the firm's boundaries. This means that HRM must ensure that individuals who are not members of the organization know what to do to contribute to the work of the firm, receive adequate feedback on the effectiveness of their actions, and are motivated to engage in co-production.

**Complementing human capital** refers to combining different resources into higher-order capabilities. At the individual level this can be achieved by (a) designing tasks and projects to make the best use of individual capabilities; (b) matching employees' capabilities to the requirements of the tasks and projects; and (c) using technology to multiply and enhance individual capabilities. Complementing human capital at the organizational level can be achieved by (a) designing organizational structures and processes, communications infrastructures, and support systems that integrate individual tasks into efficient, flexible, and responsive organizational processes; (b) combining individual and organization skills in new ways to create higher-order organizational capabilities; (c) using organizational mechanisms and communications technology to improve internal coordination and collaboration; and (d) multiplying the capabilities of the organization with advanced processes, systems, and technology. Each of these actions calls on the expertise of HRM professionals.

**Enhancing human capital** refers to improving the quality of the resource. At the individual level this can be achieved by encouraging and facilitating individual learning and by providing opportunities for training, skill development, and practice. Policies that offer financial reimbursement to employees when they attain degrees or attend conferences encourage individuals to invest in their own development. Human capital can be enhanced at the organizational level by encouraging and facilitating organizational learning and by the widespread sharing of knowledge and market intelligence. Internal "innovation fairs" or "decision spaces" devoted to the open and widespread discussion of controversial issues encourage this type of enterprise learning.

**Conserving human capital** refers to retaining the quantity and quality of the resource. At the individual level it can be achieved through the implementation of well-designed safety and retention programs. Conserving human capital at the organizational level can be achieved by implementing standard processes and routines, thus enabling the firm to accomplish the same results with less labor. For example, over-learning core activities (such as drawing prototype schematics), so that they become habits, can enable an organization to devote a greater proportion of its human capital to unfamiliar or unstructured activities (such as prototype development) that may create more significant value. Conservation also includes using less of the firm's human capital to accomplish a given objective, because resources are drawn from other sources. For example, helping others in the supply chain manage their HR, so that these organizations provide greater value to the firm, also aids in conservation. Finally, conserving HR may rely on flex-time, telecommuting, and other arrangements that enable employees to achieve a better work-life balance and thus safeguard their inner resources for periods of high productivity or work stress.

**Recovering human capital** refers to minimizing the lag between expenditure and payback. At the individual level it can be achieved by minimizing the lag between hiring and full productivity and the lag between training and application. At the organizational level it can be achieved by minimizing the lag between implementing new technologies (for example, ERP systems) and efficiencies realized from that technology. Often, recovering organizational human capital depends on the extent of social capital and structural capital that has already been created within a firm. These foundations of relationship building will be discussed more fully in a later chapter.

To sum up, as a human capital steward, HRM professionals must enable organizations to leverage their human capital. Leveraging is about gaining the maximum productivity targeted at accomplishing desired results from individual employees and the collective human capital of an organization. Leverage is the result of concentrating, accumulating, complementing, enhancing, conserving, and recovering human capital at both the individual and organization levels.

# Why Human Capital Stewardship Is Essential

In the past, HRM has experienced a role conflict within organizations. On the one hand, HRM has viewed top management as its primary customer with the focus being on implementing strategic intentions established at the top. On the other hand, it has viewed employees, too, as primary customers, taking responsibility for their morale and well-being. At times, when trying to serve both constituents, HRM served neither one very well.

A change in perspective is needed, in part because HRM practices that emerged during the industrial revolution were based on a number of assumptions that are no longer as relevant as they once were. According to Stewart (1997), some of these obsolete assumptions are that individuals prepared for specific jobs, whether through training or formal education, and that they worked in specific jobs with clearly defined job descriptions.

1. On completion of training or education, an individual's most important choice was which company to work for, since the primary locus for career mobility was the firm rather than the profession.

2. Employers "managed" employees' careers through well-defined "career ladders," connoting both upward movement and clearly defined paths through specific job experiences.

3. Jobs, especially those with elegant titles and positional rank, were the source of power in organizations. Human resource practices, such as job evaluation, reinforced positional power (Lawler, 1986).

4. Employees stayed (mostly) with one or a few employers over their worklife.

5. Internal labor markets (that is, hiring entry-level positions from outside the organization and then following a "promote from within" practice for all non – entry level positions) characterized the operation of many large organizations.

Most of these assumptions reflected a perspective that business settings were fairly orderly and predictable. These ideas reflect the notion that firms with dominant competitive positions will tend to maintain their industry leadership and that competitive advantage comes from building on current strengths and protecting current positions. However, as we have discussed in prior chapters, the business environment in the knowledge economy reflects a very different set of conditions, and, consequently, HRM must reflect a different set of premises.

Human resource management in the knowledge economy must reflect some fundamental changes from the past (Stewart, 1997). First, individuals work on multiple projects simultaneously or a series of projects sequentially, rather than a single job. A project is any series of activities and tasks that: has a specific objective to be completed within certain specifications; has defined start and end dates; has funding limits; and consumes resources (that is, money, people, and equipment) (Kerzner, 1989). Preparation for project work is different from preparation for specific jobs. The depth and breadth of competency and expertise determine the range of projects an individual may work on during a career. In addition, since responsibilities and needs often emerge while a project is underway, communication, an understanding of group behavior, flexibility, resourcefulness, and other dynamic and interpersonal capabilities, are often as important as task-related knowledge and skills for getting the work done.

Second, training and education are continuous lifelong endeavors, and the primary career choice is not which company to work for, but whether to be a generalist or a specialist. A generalist has a broader array of human capital but not as much depth in a specific area as does a specialist. Although generalists may be less vulnerable to specific company or industry declines, specialists typically have human capital that may allow them greater bargaining power in some situations. Investments an individual makes in his or her own human capital involves a personal assessment of KSAOs and a willingness to accept risk. As Stewart (1997: 79) says, "A specialist should be willing to bet on the long-term value of his specialty, do whatever it takes to be among the very best, and take risks and seek the rewards of a more entrepreneurial career." Loyalty is not to a job or a company but to a profession or to oneself.

Third, employers don't manage careers; employees manage their own careers and take responsibility for themselves. Gone are the days of the paternalistic HR department that plots out a sequence of ever-increasing job responsibilities, leading an employee to jump through a set of "hoops" for career success within a single organization. Also gone are the days when stigma was attached to job applicants with track records of working for multiple employers, pejoratively referred to as "job hoppers." In the knowledge economy, job hoppers are the norm, and resumes with work histories including many employers may be viewed as a signal of high demand rather than as a sign of weak loyalty. As Stewart (1997: 80) says, "Rather than describe a man or woman who has had few changes of company but many changes of title, a resume will show fewer titles, but many more employers. Titles will matter little ... Resumes will tell the story of what I did for the customer. Whom I did it for is just a byproduct."

Fourth, power flows less from position and more from expertise in the knowledge economy. In fact, on one project, an individual may be the leader, whereas on the next one, he or she may be a team member. The determining factor of what role to play on a particular project will derive from competency and expertise, not seniority and job title.

Fifth, in the knowledge economy, human capital can be obtained either internally or externally. Internal labor markets, with their "promote from within" philosophies, were appropriate for bureaucratic organizations in relatively stable markets. However, in the fast-paced knowledge economy, such systems are no longer sustainable. Instead, human capital must be obtained quickly when it is needed and rapidly deployed to where it is needed. Human resource management will also be responsible for building competencies in anticipation of future developments. Given the fleeting nature of many business opportunities, it will be useless to wait until a particular project or strategic action has been selected to begin finding or developing the needed human capital. Human resource management must have such a complete and intimate understanding of the firm's strategic intent that it can design the capability packages that can be used to formulate strategic actions.

Finally, careers are made in markets, not internal labor markets. "Free agents" is a fitting metaphor for workers in the knowledge economy. Even for those who work in an organization's "core group," it is necessary to compete with alternate sources of human capital that can be obtained on the open market. Insiders must compete with other insiders as well as outsiders for spots on project teams. Human resource management must be able to assist employees not only in reconceptualizing their capabilities but also in marketing those capabilities in ways that highlight their contribution to significant organizational outcomes.

Changing assumptions about people, work, and the way work is organized and accomplished have created the need for a changed way of thinking in HRM. Traditional programs and practices will no longer suffice in the knowledge economy. New approaches to HRM that recognize and adapt to a new set of assumptions and conditions will be necessary for organizations that want to compete effectively in the long run.

So, why should HRM embrace the role of a human capital steward? A steward doesn't really "own" a resource; rather, a steward has the responsibility for sustaining, growing, and developing that resource during the time he or she is responsible for the resource. Human capital cannot be simply bought and used like other raw materials or equipment. Instead, human capital must be contributed by the employee voluntarily. As Dess and Pickens (1999) explain, four characteristics of human capital make the stewardship perspective particularly appropriate. First, human capital is not the property of an organization. Unlike buildings or machinery, it is essentially "rented" from the employee on a daily basis. Second, human capital does not depreciate in the traditional sense. Human capital can become obsolete or irrelevant to a firm's current purpose, but it can also be continuously renewed so that it appreciates rather than diminishes in value over time. Third, human capital is a work in process. It is dynamic, and while it may not be infinitely expansible like knowledge, it can be developed and improved throughout an employee's lifetime. Likewise it can be squandered and wasted throughout an employee's lifetime. Fourth, human capital development is only limited by such factors as disease, age, or fatigue, but not in the same way as physical limitations precluded industrial age workers from continuing to work once they had lost some of their physical capabilities.

According to some, such as Baruch Lev (2002), the failure to assume a human capital stewardship role offers a partial explanation for the cascade of problems Arthur Andersen experienced as a result of their relationship with Enron prior to its failure. As with most big accounting firms, the trend over the past decade has been to reduce the recruiting of expensive MBAs and to focus instead on hiring accounting undergraduates and even, on occasion, promising liberal arts students. At the same time these accounting firms often retire their auditors at an early age by most standards, usually during an auditor's fifties. The result is a net erosion of expertise and experience that has seriously reduced the human capital in these firms. Although large accounting firms still have many highly qualified people working for them, some question whether they have the widespread organizational capability needed to audit enterprises in the complex knowledge economy. Enron engaged in business practices that were far from routine and familiar. Perhaps one explanation for Arthur Andersen's lack of effective oversight is a lack of perspective that can only be developed over time from observing both successes and failures.

Stewardship of the land, the forests, wildlife, and other natural resources is based on two underlying principles that also apply to human capital. As stewards of natural resources—park rangers, communities, and other constituents—all work together to enjoy and use the resources in the present and to create a legacy that can be passed on to future generations, likewise, human capital stewards must create, develop, and nurture the human capital of their organizations to use it productively in the present as well as to create a capacity for meeting the needs of the future. As with natural resources, stewardship of a firm's human capital is a collaborative activity.

# Chapter 4

# Knowledge Facilitator

"Knowledge sharing is considered by most people as personal decision as opposed to absolute obligation. And personal decisions to share knowledge are most sensitive to trust and goodwill."
—Ora Setter

"Knowledge management is to knowledge-based organizations what job procedures were in administration and manufacturing-based organizations."
—Allan Punzalan Isaac

*Knowledge management* has become a fashionable term in organizations today. There are even chief knowledge officers (CKOs), although individuals in this role frequently find themselves having to explain what their job titles mean. Just what is meant by "knowledge" and how one might "manage" it is a frequent topic of discussion. In this chapter, we will first define knowledge and knowledge management. Then, we will describe a new role for HRM—that of **knowledge facilitator**—and what it entails.

Next, we will discuss some of the HR challenges involved in managing knowledge.

Knowledge management may sound like the latest management fad, following in the steps of total quality management (TQM) and business process reengineering. However, although the term may be new and trendy, the concept is as old as the pyramids of Giza.

Dr. Robert E. Neilson imagined what it must have been like on a construction crew for the pyramids in 2400 B.C. (Neilson, 2001: 35):

> Referring to his papyrus blueprints and sand table model, the chief architect begins: "we are going to build a pyramid that is 756 feet square in plane and 481 feet high. The angle of inclination of the triangular faces will be 51.5 degrees. The base will cover about 13 acres and I estimate this pyramid will consist of 2,300,000 dressed stones averaging 2.5 tons each.
>
> After much trial and error trying to pull 2.5-ton blocks of sandstone over the desert sands, you learn that putting logs underneath the stone blocks and using ramps saves on the back muscles. This knowledge is passed on to other work crews. As crew members are transferred to other jobs or recruited to fight in the Pharaoh's army, this "know-how" becomes a generally accepted practice in the pyramid and military construction business. After several decades of hard work, you and your

compatriots finish construction ahead of schedule and below cost estimates.

From the story, we can learn several things about what is meant by knowledge and knowledge management. First, what is knowledge? Alan Burton-Jones (1999: 5) defines knowledge as "the cumulative stock of information and skills derived from use of information by the recipient." Similarly, Leonard and Sensiper (1998: 112) defines knowledge as "information that is relevant, actionable, and at least partially based on experience." **Knowledge** is information that is linked to potential actions because an individual is able to use it. In contrast, **data** are any signals that can be sent by an originator to a recipient (human or otherwise), whereas **information** is data that are intelligible to the recipient. In our pyramid example, data may include the temperature: 120 degrees. Information puts the data into a context: 120 degrees is so hot that men get exhausted quickly. Knowledge may include: It is more productive to haul stones early in the early morning or late in the day, when it is cooler.

The "knowledge capital" of an organization can be identified in its human capital (workforce), customer capital (customer demands and preferences), and its structural capital (systems, processes, and products) (Burton-Jones, 1999). In our example, the workers, supervisors, architects, and engineers represent the human capital; the pharaoh and his family represent customer capital; and the systems and processes used to build the pyramids, such as putting logs under the stone blocks, represent the structural capital.

Second, knowledge exists in two primary forms: explicit and tacit. **Explicit knowledge** can be articulated, or codified, in the form of words, numbers, or symbols and is more easily passed on or communicated (Saint-Onge, 2001). In our pyramid example, explicit knowledge is incorporated in the papyrus blueprints and sand table model. With that explicit knowledge, the pyramids could be duplicated in different locations. Explicit knowledge is passed along in books, communicated through lectures, described in diagrams. For example, the Internet is a conduit for massive amounts of explicit knowledge transfer, some that can be used for good (such as medical knowledge on steps patients can take to reduce the risk of Type II diabetes), some that can be used for evil (such as mechanical and chemical knowledge on steps to construct a bomb).

**Tacit knowledge** is an individual's intuitions, beliefs, assumptions, and values formed as a result of experience, and the inferences the individual draws from that experience (which may be difficult to communicate) (Saint-Onge, 1998). Tacit knowledge forms a mental grid in the background of a person's mind; it acts as a filter through which new experiences are understood and interpreted. Tacit knowledge is often explained through the phrase "people know a lot more than they realize"; they develop huge repertoires of skills, information, and ways of working that they have internalized to the point of obliviousness (Stewart, 1997). Organizations, too, possess tacit knowledge: intuitions, rules of thumb, mind-sets, unwritten rules of turf and territory, and unconscious values—much of that which makes up corporate culture. Tacit knowledge is automatic and requires little time or thought: For example, typing and riding a bicycle are much faster and much less prone to error when done without thinking or watching one's movements.

Third, both explicit and tacit knowledge can be managed. In the example, the pyramid construction workers were encouraged to share what they learned about how to move stone blocks with other crews. Crews were kept together (early forms of communities of practice) and shared knowledge and developed norms of behavior among themselves as they gained experience. Since tacit knowledge is difficult to articulate, it is often shared best through observation or by becoming involved in a situation. One crew might learn, for example, that Ashok was strong but not good with details, so he was best assigned to pulling the ropes rather than tying them, and that Zed was unusually persuasive so he should be the one to ask for water. This information would be unique to that group of workers. Another crew might learn from a spilled goatskin that putting water on the ground in front of the stones helped them slide easier. This information might be observed by other crews working in close proximity and passed along the crews like a ripple on a pond. Knowledge sharing both sped up construction progress and increased worker life expectancy. We don't know whether the lessons learned by crews were transferred to other construction projects; if the lessons weren't transferred, subsequent projects would have steep learning curves and needless deaths.

Fourth, HRM can play a facilitative role in knowledge management. In our example, workers were encouraged to share innovative ideas that improved productivity. Imagine how different it would have been, had our pyramid workers been punished for suggesting alternative ways of doing things; squashing ideas *and workers*. Keeping crews together created an opportunity for team learning. And allowing teams to share what they learned with other teams encouraged best practices to be diffused quickly throughout the pyramid-building workforce. Imagine how different it would have been, had crews been formed and re-formed on a daily basis, preventing cohesion, and if those crews had not been allowed to communicate with other crews, hindering or eliminating the capacity to transfer knowledge. Human resource management can play a crucial role in both training and direct facilitation of these aspects of knowledge management. It can reiterate and demonstrate the importance of sharing new ideas quickly and effectively. It can design organizational structures and processes that promote knowledge diffusion. It can help firms develop timelines for employee transfer that capitalize on familiarity and group cohesion and also recognize the benefits of broad ties and diversity of experience.

# Why Manage Knowledge?

When people say they are "managing" knowledge, what does that imply? The classical definition of management refers to planning, organizing, staffing, directing, coordinating, reporting, and budgeting. Updated definitions include terms such as coaching, mentoring, and leading. Can knowledge be managed like other resources? Well, yes and no.

Bob Buckman prefers the term "leveraging knowledge," since "managing" is an industrial age term that is too related to the word "control" (Buckman, 1997). Part of the difficulty in labeling derives from how people view knowledge management (Sveiby, 1998). Two different views have emerged: an object view of knowledge and a process view of knowledge. The **knowledge as object** view is common among those who have education in computer and/or information science. They view knowledge as objects that can be identified and handled in information systems. They focus on databases or other storage devices, and mechanisms for sharing knowledge products, such as documents, and they use such terms as "knowledge transfer." For individuals with the object view, managing knowledge means manipulating the electronic signals or other representations. On the other hand, the **knowledge as process** view is common among those who have education in philosophy, psychology, sociology, or business management. They view knowledge as the outcome of a learning process and are involved primarily in assessing, changing, and improving human individuals' skills and/or behavior by facilitating collaboration, learning, and problem solving, and they use such terms as "communities of practice." For individuals with a process view, managing knowledge means orchestrating the stream of activities that results in understanding and insight. But to truly manage or leverage knowledge, it is necessary both to manage objects and to manage processes: a difficult challenge when each is considered separately and a formidable challenge when both are considered simultaneously.

Why must knowledge be managed? What's to be gained by managing knowledge? What's to be lost if knowledge isn't managed effectively? The answer is clear: By actively managing knowledge, rather than letting knowledge-related activities run their own course, organizations can experience many positive and desirable outcomes. For example, Stewart (1997) identifies the following reasons for managing knowledge: rapid knowledge sharing, collective knowledge growth, shortened lead times, and more productive people. Fell (2001) has identified five major benefits of knowledge management (see Table 4.1).

Table 4.1 Benefits of Knowledge Management

| Benefits of Knowledge Management | Why Benefits Occur |
|---|---|
| Knowledge management can create competitive advantage for a company and its customers. | • By sharing information and best practices, organizations create expanded opportunities for market share and financial growth.<br>• Furthermore, knowledge management provides a means for organizations to differentiate themselves from competitors. |
| Knowledge management can create a truly customer-focused culture. | • Appropriate organizational resources can be directed toward solving customer problems or meeting customer needs quickly and effectively. |
| Knowledge management can be a catalyst. | • Through tools, resources, and systems, it can help ignite creativity and innovation in the development of an organization's products and services. |
| Knowledge management can improve time to market. | • By leveraging best practices, learning, and other time-savers to improve productivity, products can be introduced faster. |
| Knowledge management can expand a company's strategic options. | • By leveraging intellectual property in research and development efforts as well as overall market and business strategy, organizations can discover new ways to create value. |

- Knowledge management can create competitive advantage for a company and its customers. By sharing information and best practices, organizations create expanded opportunities for market share and financial growth. Furthermore, knowledge management provides a means for organizations to differentiate themselves from competitors.

- Knowledge management can create a truly customer-focused culture. Appropriate organizational resources can be directed toward solving customer problems or meeting customer needs quickly and effectively.

- Knowledge management can be a catalyst to create tools, resources, and systems to help ignite creativity and innovation in the development of an organization's products and services.

- Knowledge management can improve time to market by leveraging best practices, learning, and other time-savers to improve productivity.

- Knowledge management can expand a company's strategic options by leveraging intellectual property in research and development efforts as well as overall market and business strategy.

Knowledge management allows organizations to respond effectively to threats, problems, and other changes in the marketplace. Buckman

Laboratories found that a customer needing a solution to a problem in France was able to get one from an associate in Monaco after receiving input from U.S. associates and locating previous solutions and presentations on the K'netix knowledge network (Hackett, 2000). Another Buckman associate (that is, employee) had a microbiological control problem that was solved by a colleague halfway around the globe who had a hobby (microbrewing), which involved controlling a similar organism. In both cases, rapid knowledge sharing led to more productive people who solved customers' problems quickly. This capability resulted in big gains for the company.

Knowledge management allows an organization to be proactive in identifying new markets and opportunities. Successful metanational organizations prospect and assess potentially valuable technologies and market knowledge from around the world (Doz, Santos, & Williamson, 2001). Polygram, the record company, built an organization capable of identifying future global hit artists through knowledge management. They found local talent in bars and nightclubs from cities as widespread as São Paulo, Reykjavík, Naples, Paris, Athens, and Hong Kong. Using their knowledge of international music markets, Polygram was able to become the world's largest record company.

Knowledge management serves to leverage human capital, both for the organization and for individual employees. In Buckman Laboratories, individuals who used the knowledge network most successfully are identified as "power users." They are viewed by the company as having utilized the knowledge management tools to increase their span of communication, which enhanced their influence over a wider span of the organization. It is a win-win situation: These power users are able to move the organization forward, demonstrate their value to the organization, and obtain greater responsibility when the opportunities arise (Martinez, 1998).

Unless knowledge is actively managed, it may not be captured in ways that apply what is known to resolve organizational challenges. For example, the U.S. Army does not want to leave it to chance that lessons learned from field exercises will be accurately interpreted, transmitted, and turned into improved behaviors. Thus, the Army has developed the after-action review (AAR) process that immediately debriefs, documents, and shares insights from field experience. Without this formal process, many useful observations and good ideas are likely to remain unnoticed. The AAR, or other forms of "action learning," ensures that the knowledge quickly and pervasively becomes part of the organization's intellectual capital.

All in all, knowledge management can provide an organization with many benefits. Organizations can more effectively counter problems and threats and can respond more proactively to opportunities. In a knowledge-based economy, managing knowledge along with other resources is a requirement, not an option.

# What Is Knowledge Management?

As was apparent from our pyramid example, one doesn't need cell phones, computers, the Internet, or other sophisticated technologies to manage knowledge. But with such technology, possibilities for managing knowledge that were heretofore unimagined become realities. Today, when we think about knowledge management, most of us conjure up images of sophisticated intranet and Internet applications. Consequently, definitions of knowledge management usually imply, if not state, technology links.

Knowledge management has been defined in many ways. And while there is commonality among the definitions, each emphasizes something different. Here are some examples.

- Knowledge management is "the identification, optimization, and active management of intellectual assets, either in the form of explicit knowledge held in artifacts or as tacit knowledge possessed by individuals or communities" (Snowden, 1998). Knowledge management is "the leveraging of collective wisdom to increase responsiveness and innovation" (Cortada & Woods, 1999).
- Knowledge management is "the discipline that promotes an integrated approach to

identifying, capturing, retrieving, sharing, and evaluating an enterprise's information assets. These information assets may include databases, documents, policies, and procedures as well as uncaptured, tacit expertise and experience resident in individual workers" (Neilson, 2001).

- Knowledge management "means attending to processes for creating, sustaining, applying, sharing and renewing knowledge to enhance organizational performance and create value" (Buckman, 1997).

- Knowledge management is "the practice of harnessing and exploiting intellectual capital to gain competitive advantage and customer commitment through efficiency, innovation and faster and more effective decision making" (Barth, 2000).

There are two major themes that are apparent in all of these definitions. One theme relates to acquiring and disseminating useful knowledge. Organizations must look for and gather knowledge from a variety of sources that could be useful, both internally and externally, and then disseminate what is learned to employees (and others) who can use that information. A second theme relates to applying knowledge toward the creation of competitive advantage. This second theme focuses on using knowledge and sharing knowledge to create new products and services, improve efficiencies in serving customers, and develop capabilities that lead to new sources of value creation. Perhaps both themes are best summed up in the following quote from Buckman Laboratories employee Mike Ansley (Cohen, 1997: 8):

> It is a matter of understanding how we can get as many people as possible creating and transferring as much knowledge as possible in the best way possible in order to have a positive impact on the customer. It's about bringing the full weight of the knowledge that exists in the hardware, software, and wetware (people), in a relevant and useful manner, to bear upon the requirements of the customer.

One useful way of understanding the nature of knowledge management is to separate it into two main components: stocks and flows (Stewart, 1997). **Knowledge stocks** are repositories of the collected know-how, experience, and wisdom of the organization. Knowledge stocks are databases that make it easier to tap into the knowledge of colleagues and a vast array of information that could stimulate innovation or solve a problem. Knowledge stocks also enable organizations to work globally more effectively and deliver expertise instantaneously. Stewart (1997) proposes that three major types of items should be stored in knowledge stocks: corporate yellow pages, lessons learned, and competitor intelligence. *Corporate yellow pages* map the sources of expertise within an organization. As the name implies, you can use them like telephone yellow pages and "let your fingers do the walking" to find the right person with the right knowledge at the right time. *Lessons learned* are documents reflecting what went right and what went wrong in completing a task or a project, along with guidelines for those undertaking similar assignments. At General Motors, field technicians are provided with voice-driven personal computers, which they wear on their belts to describe their repair procedures aloud (Burton-Jones, 1999). Their voices are converted into text instantaneously. The company intends to collect this information from the technicians on an intranet, assess the information at headquarters, and then adjust service procedures and training manuals rapidly as new lessons are learned. *Competitor intelligence* includes knowledge about competitors' products, processes, finances, and employment activities. Much of this knowledge can be accessed quickly and efficiently from the Internet and from annual reports, published newsletters, or other public documents. For example, some firms in the Silicon Valley routinely review employment sections of the local newspapers and *The Wall Street Journal* to gain clues regarding competitors' product development directions from the kinds of human talent that rivals are seeking. However, precautions must be observed in obtaining and using competitor intelligence (Warren, 2002).

Accuracy regarding the data itself, as well as its interpretation, is difficult to assess. Corporate yellow pages, lessons learned, and competitor intelligence provide core knowledge stocks that can be supplemented with additional stocks of knowledge useful to a particular organization.

**Knowledge flows** are movements of knowledge between individuals, across departments and functions, and among suppliers and distributors. In the paper-based world of twentieth-century business, companies often had slow and ponderous mechanisms for moving knowledge around. Reports, forms, and other tangible records of knowledge flowed through rulebound hierarchies, oftentimes getting to the right people at the wrong time. Technology has enabled knowledge flows to occur instantaneously, so that individuals who need the information get it when they need it and when they can use it. And although technology has speeded knowledge flows, companies have also incorporated more low-tech approaches to dissemination, as well. For example, Xerox organizes "Teamwork Day," in which teams from purchasing, manufacturing, sales, engineering, and customer service meet in a convention center, set up booths, and tell each other what they are doing and what they have learned (Stewart, 2000). Intranets, the Internet, and "peoplenets" form the arteries for knowledge flows.

It is important to note, however, that the increased and pervasive knowledge flows, which advanced technology permits, are not always beneficial. Whereas the primary complaint in the industrial era was insufficient information on which to make informed decisions, one of the dominant concerns in the knowledge economy is *information overload,* in which sorting through an excessive avalanche of incoming data for relevant and reliable information is the most pressing concern. Post hoc analyses of the 9/11 terrorist attacks on the United States suggest that massive amounts of information were available, but sorting and analyzing it in time to prevent the attack was a major challenge that ultimately proved unsuccessful. As a result of information overload, critical thinking, decision framing, and other analytic and judgmental aspects of human capital must play a crucial role in effective knowledge management.

Davenport and Prusak (1998) have identified a four-stage process of knowledge management that encompasses both building knowledge stocks and facilitating knowledge flows. Although the stages are described in a step-by-step sequential fashion, the researchers acknowledge that the process is really fluid and open. The four stages of the knowledge management process are as follows.

1.  **Creation and acquisition:** In this stage, organizations obtain the knowledge they need. This knowledge can be acquired in three primary ways. First, an organization

can buy needed knowledge. When firms buy other firms, they purchase human capital, structural capital, and customer capital. Structural capital is purchased by obtaining knowledge about processes and routines or by buying the technology system that contains the know-how from vendors. However, human capital resides in the employees, and customer capital resides in relationships between the organization and its customers. Thus, a crucial component of effective knowledge management is the identification of key employees who have essential knowledge. These employees must be convinced to stay with the firm and to share what they know. Organizations must also identify key customers and convince them to stay, as well. Second, an organization can rent needed knowledge. This is related to Ulrich's (1998) and to Hamel and Prahalad's (1993) borrowing strategies discussed in the previous chapter. Hiring consultants and professors is one way to rent their knowledge. And if the organization ensures a mechanism for knowledge transfer, this rented knowledge can become "owned." And third, organizations can develop needed knowledge. For example, Chaparral Steel encourages all employees to think of new ways to do things and new ways to work. Chaparral also offers their employees educational sabbaticals to enable them to concentrate on knowledge acquisition and to reinforce the notion of life-long learning. Chaparral Steel is intent on developing its own knowledge to protect their competitive uniqueness.

2. **Codification:** The purpose of codification is to make local and often tacit knowledge explicit and available for wide distribution. Snowden (1998) describes this as moving explicit knowledge from individuals to communities, changing tacit knowledge to make it explicit, and then moving the formerly tacit knowledge from individuals to communities. Efforts to codify knowledge may take many forms. For example, a worker may document a procedure he or she used, then the documentation is posted on the knowledge database. Retiring company experts may be videotaped to capture their knowledge in a form that others can learn from, in the same way that many film documentarians use this technique. Firms may invest in information technologies such as ERP systems, in which business processes and information flows

run in parallel. Many different types of knowledge can be codified, including individual knowledge, organizational networks, algorithms developed by communities of practice, heuristics for project teams, competencies and capabilities, processes, and events.

3. **Distribution:** The purpose of distribution is to make knowledge available to those who need it and can use it. Groupware, knowledge bases, and intranets are dominant methods of distribution. Making knowledge accessible not only requires easy access but also convenient and understandable sorting. Effective knowledge distribution includes mechanisms for cataloging and categorizing data, so that relevant information can be identified in a timely manner. This process is analogous to library catalogs or phone book indexes that allow people to find what they need in a user-friendly manner. Human resource management can contribute to the design of people-sensitive systems and to training in their usage.

4. **Use:** Knowledge must be applied to solving problems and creating new ideas if it is to have any influence on a firm's competitive position. Knowledge that is created, codified, and distributed, but not used, is like having

a library full of unread books. Merely making knowledge available is not enough. Although you can lead a horse to water, you can't make it drink. Attention must be drawn to the knowledge, and an appetite must be created for acquiring and sharing knowledge. People must understand what information is potentially useful to them and how it should be applied. Knowledge at rest is not knowledge that is making a difference. Hiring employees who are adept knowledge users is one way to get knowledge applied to serve organizational purposes. Organizations can also create roles for individuals charged with bringing relevant knowledge into a project. As with capitalizing on any other resource, HRM must develop ways to ensure that individuals take full advantage of the organizational assets that are available to them. This includes developing the motivation, competencies, value orientation, and knowledge of the firm's strategic intent necessary to use knowledge to enhance organizational capabilities.

A recent conference of experts summarized their observations on knowledge management in the following points (Cohen, 1997: 5). First, "knowledge is an organizational asset that must be systematically valued, nourished, shared, and used." Effective knowledge management is vital to competing in the global economy today. Second, "because knowledge is rooted in human experience and social context, managing it well means paying attention to people, culture, and organizational structure, as well as to the technology that is an essential tool for knowledge sharing and use in large organizations." And third, "successful knowledge management may require fundamental and lasting changes in the way organizations operate internally and how they do business with their customers and partners." It is clear from these three conclusions that HRM has the opportunity to play a significant role in knowledge management in organizations (see Table 4.2).

Table 4.2 Human Resource Management and the Knowledge Management Process

| Knowledge Management Stage | Definition | HR Actions |
| --- | --- | --- |
| Creation and Acquisition | Organizations obtain the knowledge they need by buying, renting, or developing it. | • Identify sources of knowledge. |
| | | • Serve as intermediary in acquiring knowledge. |
| | | • Serve as facilitator in developing knowledge. |
| Codification | Make local and often tacit knowledge explicit and available for wide distribution. | • Identify relevant knowledge to capture. |

| | | • Use multiple means (videotape, documentation, and so on) to capture knowledge. |
| Distribution | Make knowledge available to those who need it and can use it. | • Design people-sensitive systems for knowledge distribution. |
| | | • Train users how to access information. |
| Use | Knowledge is applied to solving problems and creating new ideas. | • Make information access points user friendly. |
| | | • Reward users. |

# Human Resource Management as Knowledge Facilitator

Why must HRM assume the role of knowledge facilitator? There are several reasons. First, others in organizations (information technology professionals, in particular) are filling the void, and they may not have the competencies and capabilities to focus on the human element in knowledge management. They may be experts in databases and information systems, but it doesn't follow that they will also be experts in "people systems." Designing technical information systems that do not reflect the ways in which people actually obtain, interpret, distribute, or use information is one of the most common sources of technical information systems failure (Davenport, 2000). As Thomas Stewart (1997: 139) describes it, "the role of technology is to support the real knowledge network—the informal one of people talking to people." Human resource management can focus on this informal network of people talking to people. As Barney (1995) explains, for a resource to be fully exploitable, a firm must design its architecture, control systems, compensation practices, and relationships to serve as complementary resources. In addition, information storage and transfer technologies are often broadly dispersed within an industry as vendors often determine best practices and build their assessment into the systems they sell. The ways in which knowledge is used, and the social capital gains that can result, are much more difficult to replicate and therefore can provide a much more compelling source of competitive advantage.

Second, knowledge management goes beyond the traditional HRM function of training and development. Knowledge management integrates HR directly into the value-adding processes of a business. Knowledge management creates organizational capabilities that are directly tied to specific sources of value creation. For example, Wal-Mart's point-of-purchase inventory management system technology has been largely imitated by K-Mart. However, Wal-Mart's knowledge management practices enabled them to more effectively exploit the data such a system provides, so that individual store managers throughout their network use the data to make informed local choices about purchasing, marketing, displays, and so forth in ways that capitalize on the information resource. Human resource management's role in helping Wal-Mart employees effectively use the knowledge made available by the technical system to make better, faster, and more locally sensitive decisions is the root source of its advantage. K-Mart has not developed this capability, and, as has been seen, the competitive outcomes are dramatically different. The difference is the way that people use knowledge. Therefore, as a knowledge facilitator, HRM has the opportunity to have a clear impact on the bottom line.

Third, as more organizations develop formal knowledge management programs, they must often make major cultural changes and behavioral adjustments if they are to benefit from the investment. Human resource management should be a primary change-agent in organizations (Ulrich, 1998). As a change-agent, HRM has the opportunity to help organizations adapt to the rapidly shifting environments they confront. This means that HRM must take an active part in shaping the culture and designing the processes that enable a firm to transform itself. Both as change-agent and as a role model, HRM must create a firm's capacity for continuous change. If a firm is not able to alter its behavior as a result of what it learns, then knowledge has little value.

And finally, knowledge management calls for a flexible and holistic approach, integrating factors of organizational culture, technology, and goals. Integration will not happen by chance—and few functions in the organization have a broad enough perspective to make it happen. Human resource management is in a position to provide the organizational "glue" to link these elements together. People provide the platform for integration of ideas and actions across the enterprise and people are the primary target for HRM work.

What are the expectations of HRM in the role of knowledge facilitator. (See Table 4.3.) First, HR should help the organization articulate the purpose of the knowledge management system. Mark Koskiniemi of Buckman Labs (Koskiniemi, 2001) boils it down to a simple fill-in-the-blank statement: "Our knowledge management initiatives help _____ (who) get _____ (what) to accomplish _____ (goal)." For example, "Our knowledge management initiatives help our field representatives get access to real world success stories to accomplish our goal of increasing profitable sales." This sounds a little bit like management by objectives, doesn't it? That is precisely the role HRM must play to ensure that knowledge management initiatives actually deal with important issues. Investing in a knowledge management initiative without a clear sense of purpose is like investing in an expensive camera that has far more capabilities than you need to take good pictures of family and friends. Too often, organizations embrace technologies to solve problems before they've even identified the problems they are trying to solve. Then, once they realize the error, they find it difficult to abandon the original solution and difficult to gather the resources needed to invest in a solution to the real problem. Effectively framing the knowledge management issue, before deciding on a course of action, is a crucial prerequisite for success.

Table 4.3 How Human Resource Management Can Facilitate Knowledge Management

1. HRM can help the organization articulate the purpose of the knowledge management system.

2. HRM can ensure alignment among an organization's mission, statement of ethics, and policies: These should all be directed toward creating an environment of sharing and using knowledge with a full understanding of the competitive consequences.

3. HRM can help create the "ultimate employee experience." That is, by transforming tacit knowledge into explicit knowledge through education, it can help build employee skills, competencies, and careers, creating "bench strength."

4. HRM can integrate effective knowledge sharing and usage into daily life.

5. HRM must relax controls and allow (even encourage) behaviors that, in the clockwork world of industrial efficiency, never would have been tolerated.

6. HRM can take a strategic approach to helping firms manage email, Instant Messenger, Internet surfing, and similar technologies.

7. HRM can champion low-tech solutions to knowledge management.

Second, as a knowledge facilitator, HRM must ensure alignment among an organization's mission, statement of ethics, and policies: These should all be directed toward creating an environment of sharing and using knowledge with full understanding of the competitive consequences. Buckman Laboratories, for example, has the following mission.

We, the associates of Buckman Laboratories, will excel in providing measurable, cost-effective improvements in output and quality for our customers by delivering customer-specific services and products, and the creative application of knowledge.

In addition to their mission, Buckman's code of ethics emphasizes the respect and trust that are necessary for creating a knowledge-sharing environment. However, the boundaries are also clear. Buckman employees must share knowledge with each other and with the particular client for which a service is being developed, but they must also preserve clients' ability to protect their knowledge-based advantages from rivals. Human resource management must also ensure that executives and managers alike are behaving in ways consistent with the mission, code of ethics, and policies that enable appropriate knowledge sharing; executives and managers must *both* "talk the talk and walk the walk." Furthermore, HRM must nourish a culture that embraces getting the right information to the right people at the right time (Fell, 2001).

Third, Fell (2001) advocates HRM to create the "ultimate employee experience." That is, by transforming tacit knowledge into explicit knowledge through education, organizations must build employee skills, competencies, and careers, creating "bench strength." This combines the traditional training and development responsibilities of HRM with the new responsibilities of human capital steward: using all of the organization's resources to create strategic capability. Disney's new staff orientation, which emphasizes the firm's mission, values, and history within a context of the "magic kingdom" experience, is an example of this process of making tacit knowledge more visible.

Fourth, HRM must integrate effective knowledge sharing and usage into daily life (Cohen, 1997). That is, knowledge sharing must be expected, recognized, and rewarded. For many individuals and organizations, this reverses the conventional relationship between knowledge and power. Often, the common pattern was to hoard knowledge because it made the individual more valuable and more difficult to replace. Effective knowledge management requires this trend to be overturned and requires those with information to become teachers and mentors who ensure that others in the firm know what they know. Teaching must become part of everyone's job. Clearly, for such a cultural shift to take place, HRM must overhaul selection, appraisal, and compensation practices. Human resource management has the capabilities for creating, measuring, and reinforcing a knowledge-sharing expectation.

Fifth, HRM must relax controls and allow (even encourage) behaviors that, in the clockwork world of industrial efficiency, never would have been tolerated. For example, conversations at the water cooler were viewed in the past as unproductive uses of employee time—after all, employees were not at their desks completing specified tasks detailed in their job descriptions (Davenport & Prusak, 1999). In the knowledge economy, "conversations inside and outside the company are the chief mechanism for making change and renewal an ongoing part of the company's culture" (Webber, 1993: 7). As another example, consider individuals in organizations described as "gossips," who would rather talk than work. Frederick Taylor's industrial engineers would have eliminated these gossips from workplaces in the early twentieth century, since they did nothing that was perceptibly valuable. However, in the knowledge economy, if the conversations are relevant to the firm's strategic intent, these same people may be described as "knowledge brokers": those individuals who like to move around the company to hear what is going on, sparking new knowledge creation by carrying ideas between groups of people who do not communicate directly. If the topics serve organizational needs, these individuals play a role similar to bees that cross-pollinate flowers and sustain a larger ecosystem. Organizations should selectively recognize and reward, rather than universally discourage and punish, these types of behaviors. Clearly, not all conversation is productive and constructive. Human resource management still must play a role in discouraging gossip that undermines, rather than promotes, a learning community. Human resource management will need to adjust both its own perspective (from rule-enforcer) as well as that of managers and others who hold outdated notions of what is "real work."

Sixth, HRM must take a strategic approach to helping firms manage email, Instant Messenger, Internet surfing, and similar uses of technology. Clearly, the Internet has a role in generating and disseminating knowledge, and therefore is an integral part of knowledge management. But what are the unintended effects of monitoring email, tracking employees' Web searches, and similar issues related to privacy? Certainly some control is needed, but the larger question for HRM is determining appropriate boundaries. When does control become counterproductive? When does excessive monitoring become an inappropriate invasion of privacy? A related issue is HRM's role in helping firms manage the distancing consequences of electronic communication. As employees increasingly rely on technology to communicate, they lose opportunities to develop the rich, multifaceted relationships that encourage the communication of tacit knowledge. Human resource management can contribute to developing social capital by sensitizing employees to the negative consequences of excessive reliance on electronic media and by creating opportunities for face-to-face contact.

Seventh, HRM must champion the low-tech solutions to knowledge management. Although it should not ignore the high-tech knowledge management tools, HRM contains the expertise to develop low-tech knowledge management strategies. For example, when the team that developed the Dustbuster vacuum tool was created, they were given a "war room" in which they could spread out their materials and leave sketches, models, notes, and so on plastered on walls and throughout the workspace (Cohen, 1997). These visible outputs of their thinking processes helped create a shared context for their efforts and turned the room into a truly collaborative workspace. Some Asian firms, such as Dai-Ichi, create special rooms (with green tea and comfortable places to sit), where researchers are expected to spend a half-hour daily, telling whomever they meet about their current work. Neither of the two preceding examples requires large financial investments in technology that will rapidly become obsolete. Yet both examples demonstrate how HRM could help a firm orchestrate and facilitate knowledge sharing.

As can be seen from the previous discussion, the knowledge facilitator role cannot be easily slotted into traditional HRM functions, such as training and development or compensation. The knowledge facilitator role is much more broad and requires creative integration across traditional HRM activities. It entails both rethinking old ways of managing the workplace as well as using innovative approaches outside the box of traditional HRM. Most important, becoming an effective knowledge facilitator requires conceptualizing HRM as a vehicle for creating capabilities and capitalizing on the human factor to create a community of knowledge workers.

The knowledge facilitator role is important to organizational success in the knowledge economy. When this role is performed effectively, it results in many positive outcomes (Huang, 1998). Time is used more efficiently: By leveraging the knowledge gained from experience, employees can add value to customers sooner. Furthermore, individual employees can expand and update their own human capital more quickly. Customer satisfaction is enhanced: The most current best practices can be obtained instantaneously and used to tailor-fit solutions for customers. Resources can be used more efficiently: Time saved by reusing proven solutions can be invested in other productive endeavors. Finally, new business can be generated: Interactions with customers can result (both more rapidly and more effectively) in discovering new solutions, new products, and new services.

On the other hand, when the knowledge facilitator role is performed poorly, a number of negative consequences ensue. Mistakes are repeated. This results in greater costs and slower response times as well as increasing frustration. An overdependence on a few key individuals places the organization's fate in the hands of a few rather than the hands of many. Work is duplicated, resulting in waste and inefficiency. Good ideas are bottled up and not shared, preventing the organization from adapting and adjusting to environmental changes. Finally, market entry for new products and services is delayed—a death knell in this fast-paced economy.

# Human Resource Management Challenges for the Knowledge Facilitator Role

In the industrial era, organizations used co-location (that is, bringing all employees together under "one roof") as a means to ensure that knowledge was available and accessible when needed. Co-location of the key people who drive innovation is a practice used today by firms such as Microsoft. Their corporate office in Washington houses all of their major developmental activities so that team members can communicate and solve problems in face-to-face meetings. When Microsoft buys companies to purchase their knowledge, people are brought from the acquired company to the Microsoft campus.

Co-location offers many benefits to knowledge management (Doz, Santos, & Williamson, 2001). It offers the ultimate in "high bandwidth" communication. Two-way face-to-face discussion provides a rich medium for communication. Nuances in tone, body language, and facial expressions can impart more information more effectively than, for example, email (even when "emoticons" are used!). Feedback from the recipient can be more accurately gauged and communication breakdowns can be more easily averted in face-to-face communication. Co-location increases the frequency of interaction among workers. Communication is not confined to discrete message opportunities. People are available and a walk down the hall can be initiated instantaneously. Time for reflection can occur, followed by further face-to-face conversation. Co-location increases the probability of chance encounters and serendipity. Chance encounters in the hallways, at the watercooler, in the restrooms: All may lead to knowledge sharing and may have a direct impact on job and organizational performance. Working together in the same location can lead to being "in tune" and "in sync." That is, familiarity and proximity can result in common understandings and shared values, a feeling of community. Unwritten and unspoken values do not have to be repeated for clarification. Work rhythms that are synchronized can result in more effective and efficient flows of knowledge and information.

This principle of co-location hasn't been totally abandoned, but it is much more difficult to realize today than it was in the past. One major challenge for HRM as knowledge facilitator is how to obtain the same or similar benefits of co-location when knowledge and people are dispersed and co-location is not possible. What is needed is to move around knowledge, or mobilize a "package" or "carrier" of knowledge, such as a blueprint for a building. When knowledge is moved around, however, it often gets degraded, that is, it loses something in the moving. After all, the package or carrier may not capture all of the knowledge that needs to be moved. Furthermore, once the knowledge is moved, it has to be "recontextualized," that is, made to fit and be understood in a different surrounding. Wal-Mart learned this lesson when they opened their first supercenter in Argentina; they replicated stores found in the United States precisely, following a blueprint that translates anywhere in the United States. Wal-Mart found that 110-volt appliances (a standard in the United States) did not work as well in Argentina, however, where 220 volts was the norm (Doz, Santos, & Williamson, 2001).

Human resource management has a significant challenge, but also can play a significant role in ensuring that when knowledge is moved around, the best carrier is used to fit the needs of the situation. There are three types of knowledge carriers (Argote, 2000; Doz, Santos, & Williamson, 2001): information; tools, templates, models, and machines; and people. Moving information (files, spreadsheets, blueprints, text, formulas, and so on) around is the simplest, and perhaps most efficient, way to move knowledge. It is not, however, without its problems. When Boeing designed the 777 airplane, standardized information used with computer-aided design (CAD) systems dispersed among all of the relevant personnel eliminated the costly construction of mock-ups. In contrast, when the Stealth bomber was designed using similar procedures across four different companies, the cabling for the cockpit had to be redesigned three different times because not all the relevant information was actually recognized at each stage in the process. Although documentation is a useful way to capture a great deal of information in a fairly compact form, it remains context-dependent. The more HRM gains expertise in the information-context relationship, the greater the contribution it will be able to make to a firm's effective knowledge management strategies.

Moving tools, templates, models, and machines is another way of moving knowledge around. The Wal-Mart example of putting exact store replicas in international locations transfers much of the retail giant's explicit knowledge base. Along with standard operating procedures and other tangible knowledge, much can be conveyed. The use of tools, templates, and models enables the transport of a configuration of information rather than the transmittal of mere discrete ideas. Often these methods incorporate the means to use the information as well as the knowledge itself. For example, making a decision support system widely available within a firm disseminates both data and methods for analysis. However, technology is not always able to overcome the challenges of knowledge erosion and context incongruity that accompany knowledge transfer.

Finally, moving people around as knowledge carriers is similar to the model used by many religious groups that try to spread their beliefs through missionary endeavors. As with religious missionaries who are unable to adapt to local surroundings and who find themselves unable to convert others to their beliefs, however, sending knowledge emissaries requires more than drawing straws or soliciting volunteers. As Prahalad and Hamel (1990) point out, existing organizational anchors often make it difficult to effectively use people as knowledge carriers for the corporation. Exceptionally capable individuals are frequently "captured" by product affiliations or strategic business units, and their superiors are reluctant to share these human resources with others in the firm. Internal competition for resources or recognition can promote a parochial perspective that limits enterprise-wide knowledge management. Human resource management must provide both persuasive business arguments and effective inducements to overcome these barriers.

Human resource management has an obvious role in casting people as knowledge carriers. By broadening the perspective to include managing the relationships between people and the other two types of knowledge carriers (information; and templates, models, and machines) as well, HRM can play a more significant role as knowledge facilitator, rather than as simply "people facilitator."

Beyond the direct advantages associated with ease of orchestrating knowledge carriers, co-location often fosters a community in which knowledge creation and knowledge sharing are comfortable and expected. As discussed more in the next chapter, community is built on relationships.

In addition to the challenge of recreating the benefits of co-location (without proximity), there are other knowledge management challenges that HRM must confront. For example, how does one get individuals to share their knowledge with others, when by sharing their knowledge, they make themselves less valuable (or at least the perception may exist that they are less valuable)? Furthermore, how does an organization convert knowledge in the heads of employees into structural capital without creating the perception that employees are expendable after their knowledge has been codified? This has been described (albeit rather clumsily) as the "dilemma of incentivization" (Cortada & Woods, 1999: 492). The knowledge provider (that is, the individual employee), while able to provide knowledge typically has no incentive to do so. The knowledge seeker (that is, the organization) is highly incentivized to receive the knowledge but is unable to do so without the cooperation of the knowledge provider. Some companies are trying to use traditional financial rewards focused on desired behaviors (such as knowledge sharing), but most acknowledge that more is needed than a financial inducement. A culture of trust and cooperation, along with a focus on intrinsic and extrinsic rewards, seems necessary: This represents a shift in traditional HR thinking and in organizational culture.

Laurence Prusak (Cohen, 1997) describes the challenge as related to a "market for knowledge," one in which individuals will not "sell" their knowledge unless they get some value in return. The value individuals receive may be in part financial, for example, by including knowledge sharing on performance reviews and linking them to salaries and bonuses. The value individuals receive must also include respect and reciprocation, however: By giving people responsibilities and opportunities to grow and learn, they will be motivated to invest their efforts in the organization.

Salz (2001) suggests that in order to create the free flow of knowledge and the creation of new knowledge, organizations need to create a culture of caring. He defines *caring* in this context as "a form of serious attention and interest—the feeling that characterizes the relationship between a teacher and his student." To operationalize caring, Salz prescribes developing an incentive system that rewards workers for helping and accepting help (such as Southwest Airline's *Heroes of the Heart* awards); project debriefings that cover lessons learned by individuals and the team as a whole (such as the Army's AAR); and the creation of a new form of discourse in which managers, like film directors, encourage each employee to play his or her role with maximum focus and energy—and experiment with new ideas. Salz' prescriptions represent only some of the means by which HRM can create the culture that nourishes effective knowledge management.

Another knowledge management challenge that HRM must confront is, how does one facilitate the internal transfer of knowledge without external knowledge spillover, that is, without providing competitors with proprietary knowledge that would provide them a competitive advantage over one? For a strategic resource to provide a sustained advantage, it must be protected from imitation and appropriation. Traditionally, HR practices have relied on various kinds of nondisclosure policies and tight control over who has access to what information. In the knowledge economy, neither control method seems adequate for resolving the dilemma of maximizing internal knowledge transfer while minimizing loss of proprietary knowledge. Moreover, the basic challenge has become more complicated. If firms need to share their work beyond their conventional boundaries and include suppliers, customers, and firms creating complementary products in their processes, then they must be able to share knowledge with many external parties simply to do the work. If knowledge is a source of competitive advantage, however, not only the knowledge itself but also the context for using and creating knowledge must be protected from imitation by competitors. One of the greatest challenges for HR as knowledge facilitators is to ensure that while knowledge is shared, competitive advantage is not diluted.

Intel provides an interesting example. If Intel is to maintain its leadership in microprocessor development and ensure that the desktop rather than the Web is the primary location for managing information complexity, they must ensure that firms making the products that use their microprocessors take full advantage of their technological power. This means that these firms must have a great deal of knowledge about Intel's innovative intentions and outcomes. To maintain its leadership position, however, Intel must protect its ability to create the next technology advance. For Intel, as for many other firms, knowledge management means managing the context for knowledge as much as it means managing the knowledge itself.

Trust, respect, caring, sharing, and cooperation are not traditional foci of the HR function, but in the knowledge economy they are essential ingredients to gaining competitive advantage through knowledge management. Simply using traditional HRM solutions (for instance, paying them for their knowledge) is not enough to create the complex habitat that will lead to knowledge creation and dissemination. More holistic and systemic interventions are needed, and HRM must step outside its functional borders to make it happen.

## Conclusion

Bob Buckman, a leading thinker on knowledge management and someone who "practices what he preaches" with his own company, has proclaimed that, "We need to move from the use of technology to control costs to the entrepreneurial application of technology to gain competitive advantage in the marketplace." Additionally, Buckman (1997) has identified seven challenges for the future. Note that all seven challenges have implications for HRM.

1. Anybody, anywhere in the world, can contribute to the solution of any problem in the company, no matter where it occurs. How do you organize the company to recognize that fact? How do you organize people around the flow of information rather than geography?

2. The physical office as we know it today is becoming redundant to the functioning of some organizations. If the cash flow is not generated in the office and the people are not in the office, then why do we have offices? Could we not save that investment?

3. Think about communities of individuals forming around issues, dealing with the issues, disbanding, and reforming into other communities around other issues. How does one build communities of people separated by both time and space who trust each other, so that they can function effectively?

4. Speed of response to the customer is becoming of paramount importance in the competitive marketplace. How do you have the same speed of response at the furthest reaches of your company?

5. Everybody has to be engaged with the customer. If they are not effectively engaged with the customer, why are they employed?

6. The quality of the people that one hires will be critical to one's future success. If the individual ability to acquire and use knowledge is important, then the contents of the collective mind of one's associates will determine how well one can function. How will HRM respond to this need of the company? Should we be hiring more teachers?

7. If everybody is critically important to the organization's ability to close the gap with the customer, then how do we expand the minds of our associates, so that they can be the best that they can be? How do we deliver learning anytime, anywhere?

It is clear from Buckman's list that organizations are faced with, and will continue to confront, challenges associated with managing knowledge. A reactive stance may jeopardize an organization's long-term viability. A more proactive, systematic approach can yield many gains. Second- and third-generation pyramid builders would have benefited greatly (and lived longer) if knowledge obtained by their ancestors had been managed systematically rather than haphazardly.

# Chapter 5

# Relationship Builder

"Everybody on this planet is separated by only
six other people."
—John Guarre

Organizations are networks of relationships. There are many internal relationships that affect organizations, such as supervisor-employee; union-management; line-staff; mentor-protégé; and co-worker — co-worker. There are also many external relationships that affect organizations, such as those with suppliers, customers, regulators, competitors, and other stakeholders. However, HRM has traditionally focused on individuals—hiring, training, evaluating, rewarding, and other activities have mostly centered around the individual employee (Uhl-Bien, Graen, & Scandura, 2000). This is sometimes described as "having the right people in the right place at the right time doing the right things." To more accurately reflect organizational functioning, however, we might amend that statement to read "having the right people with the *right relationships* in the right place at the right time doing the right things" (Uhl-Bien, Graen, & Scandura, 2000).

Relationships are essential. Work gets done through relationships, and frequently relationships supplant job descriptions and formal reporting hierarchies. Those who study complex adaptive systems argue that managing relationships is the only way to shape the patterns that determine organizational behavior (Capra, 1996). Every organization has its informal networks—people who know each other and help each other regardless of rank, function, or job title. And while not formally condoned, all organizations (or the people who run them) know that if job descriptions were precisely adhered to and communication followed only the reporting hierarchies in an organizational chart, little would get accomplished.

Relationship building is important because it contributes to social capital. And social capital is important to the creation of competitive advantage in the knowledge economy. It has often been said that success and effectiveness in organizations depend on "what you know" and "whom you know." Human capital is concerned with what you know, whereas social capital is concerned with whom you know. Individuals who are able to link their own human capital (what they know) with that of others in relationship networks (whom they know) can leverage their own effectiveness. They can be the source of synergy. Without people working in concert, without collaboration, there is no opportunity for synergy to develop. Furthermore, relationship networks can collectively benefit organizations through sharing resources and stimulating innovation. These relationships create what is described as **social capital.**

The importance of social capital to organizational effectiveness cannot be overestimated. Consider what happened to the Chrysler Corporation after it went through a major, largely successful reorganization in the 1990s (Cohen & Prusak, 2001). Prior to the reorganization, the company had been organized around functional departments, such as emissions systems, body, steering, and so on. After the reorganization, the company was focused on processes: platforms or model types, instead of functions. Although this entailed many immediate benefits, such as speeding up the cycle of introducing new product lines, it was not without costs. Defects began cropping up in the new designs. And, disturbingly, many of these defects were caused by problems that had been successfully solved in the past. Why did this occur? The disbanded functional departments had been rich sources of communities of practice: senior engineers mentored new engineers, and knowledge was widely shared among all of them. The reorganization disrupted the social networks that had taken years to develop and had resulted in many benefits to the company. Social capital may not be visible to the naked eye, but it is a major factor in organizational success.

Social capital has been defined in many ways. The following definition is the most broad in capturing the essence of the concept: "Social capital is the goodwill available to individuals or groups. Its source lies in the structure and content of the actor's social relations. Its effects flow from the information (access, quantity, quality, relevance, and timeliness), influence (getting things done), and solidarity (cooperation and public-spiritedness) it makes available to the actors" (Adler & Kwon, 2000). Social capital is an intangible organizational asset, like human capital. Together, human capital and social capital play a large role in an organization's ability to compete.

Social capital benefits an organization in many ways (Adler & Kwon, 2000). It helps workers find jobs and creates a richer pool of recruits for firms. It facilitates interunit resource exchange and product innovation. It facilitates the creation of intellectual capital, since people are more likely to share tacit information and take intellectual risks in a supportive social environment. It facilitates cross-functional team effectiveness, since social capital enables people to see situations from perspectives that are different from their own. It reduces turnover rates, since individuals are less likely to leave a firm if they have strong, positive social connections with their co-workers. It strengthens supplier relations, regional production networks, and interfirm learning, since social capital can be the foundation for multifaceted, multidirectional, mutually beneficial relationships that extend beyond transactional exchanges.

Traditionally, HRM has had responsibility for managing relationships, although that responsibility has been narrowly conceived—and often implied rather than explicit. For example, HRM has been viewed as a monitor of supervisor/manager – employee relationships. Human resource management has kept an eye on, but stayed out of the way of, the relationship between supervisors/managers and employees. When those relationships become problematic (for instance, a grievance is filed or a sexual harassment complaint is made), HRM has been viewed as the police, the judge, and the final arbiter. Human resource management has also played a significant role in the relationships between unions and employers.

Most of the focus of HRM has been on relationships with current employees. Current employees receive job assignments, performance appraisals, training, and rewards—HR services—to motivate, develop, and retain them. Human resource management has always had a partial relationship with retired employees, for example, by providing pensions and other benefits after the employment relationship has ended. Human resource management has always had at least a partial relationship with potential employees (applicants), though to varying degrees across organizations. With employees who have left the organization through termination (voluntary or involuntary), HRM has had a fairly limited relationship, mostly centered on exit interviews, outplacement, or similar activities intended to facilitate severing the connection. Although, in some cases (such as the aircraft manufacturing industry, where hiring is a cyclical process), HRM has maintained a relationship with former employees who had been laid off, such that once business picked up again, they could be rehired.

In the past HRM has had a lesser role in *forming* relationships and a somewhat larger role in *managing* them. Almost always, HRM has been largely responsible for employee orientation and early socialization. Organizational socialization practices attempt to form individual-organization relationships—thus, HRM has played a role in establishing that early linkage. After socialization, however, HRM has traditionally played more of a monitoring and managerial role. Most of the relationships in which HRM typically intervenes have been forged elsewhere in the firm by other individuals for purposes that most people feel have little to do with HRM issues.

Human resource management has focused on formal relationships as documented in organization charts, reporting relationships, job descriptions, and policies and procedures, but not on the organization as it oftentimes truly functions (for instance, "work arounds"). Relationships that mattered to HRM were the ones described and codified (those that Brown and Duguid, 2000, describe as "canonical" practices). Informal networks and/or groups (relationships based on factors other than job or hierarchical position) have been tolerated but not supported or encouraged, for the most part, by HRM. As enforcer of the formal relationships, in many cases HRM has even discouraged social systems that avoid formal hierarchies and relationships. Informal relationships beyond their jurisdiction have often been seen as threatening to HRM influence in the firm.

In the past HRM has had almost no interest in, or impact on, value chain relationships that extend beyond the boundaries of the firm (Lengnick-Hall & Lengnick-Hall, 1999). Suppliers, distributors, and other members of the value chain were not in the purview of a single organization's HRM responsibilities. Although one organization in the supply chain may have had superior HRM practices, rarely were those practices shared with other members. Furthermore, HRM has had virtually no relationships with the customer. We have argued elsewhere that HRM is missing opportunities for contributing to a firm's competitive advantage if they neglect customers as potential quasi workforce members.

Relationships among individuals extend beyond formal job descriptions and official reporting hierarchies in organizations (which Brown and Duguid, 2000, describe as "noncanonical" practices). Work gets done through relationships. In fact, if relationships were not so crucial, organizations, as vehicles for achieving purposeful activity, would be seen as unnecessarily cumbersome and a source of overhead adding little value to productive work. Therefore, HRM needs to broaden its perspective to focus on the whole web of relationships, informal and formal, in an organization. HRM needs to tap into this web of relationships, observe what's going on, encourage and nurture some of them, discourage some of them, and "manage" some of them for the organization's benefit. In addition, HRM needs to broaden its perspective to focus on the whole web of relationships that occur between members of the organization and those that occur outside of the firm (for instance, customers, suppliers, or regulators).

## Anatomy of Relationships

To create social capital, it is necessary to understand the "anatomy" and dynamics of relationships. By understanding the different types of relationships and what creates and sustains them, HRM can more effectively intervene as a relationship builder. Without a solid understanding of how relationships "work," efforts to influence them can only be haphazard at best and detrimental at worst.

Leonard Greenhalgh (2001) has dissected relationships like a biologist dissects frogs—to understand the different elements. His framework has drawn from several bodies of research (economics, organizational behavior, psychology, sociology, and so on). Greenhalgh's framework portrays relationships as multidimensional. Each dimension consists of several factors that are defined as continua along which a particular relationship can be profiled.

# Dimensions of Relationships

There are four major dimensions of relationships: rapport, bonding, breadth, and affinity (see Table 5.1). Although these dimensions and their associated factors apply most directly to relationships between individuals, with some modification, they also can be used to describe relationships between groups within organizations or relationships between organizations. A better understanding of the elements constituting relationships provides a foundation for enabling HRM to leverage those specific factors that shape interactions in ways creating competitive value.

**Rapport** dimensions are related to the comfort people feel in dealing with each other. Rapport is strongest when there are high levels of trust, interpersonal disclosure, empathy, acceptance, and respect. *Trust* involves being able to rely on another to take one's best interests into account. In addition, it includes an element of reliability—the ability to be counted on to do what one says one will do. *Interpersonal disclosure* is the ability to be open about one's personal life with another—telling another person things about oneself that could embarrass or hurt one if used inappropriately. This type of revealing communication is an important element in building groups into communities (Eisenberg, 1990). *Empathy* is the ability to see a situation from another person's perspective. *Acceptance* is unconditional positive regard. *Respect* is admiration for a strong value system and the will to live up to it. Rapport provides a foundation for developing deep connections.

Table 5.1   Dimensions of Relationships

**Rapport**

| | |
|---|---|
| Trust | Distrust |
| Vulnerability | Social distance |
| Strong empathy | No empathy |
| High respect | Disrespect |

**Bonding**

| | |
|---|---|
| Allies | Enemies |
| Collaboration | Competition |
| Great benefit | No benefit |

**Breadth**

| | |
|---|---|
| Unlimited | Narrow |
| Continuous | Transactional |

**Affinity**

| | |
|---|---|
| Interesting | Boring |
| A lot in common | Nothing in common |
| Strong affection | Dislike |
| Attraction | Repulsion |

*Adapted from Greenhalgh, 2001*

**Bonding** dimensions are related to how robust (that is vigorous, adaptive, and enduring) the relationship is. Bonding is strongest when the other party is an ally and a collaborator. And, even though the other party may provide one with great benefits, oftentimes a stronger bond results from greater personal sacrifice. *Alliance* is a continuum ranging from loyalty to animosity. Allies don't abandon a person for short-term gain; they will take one's side when the individual is not there to observe; and they make a public commitment to the relationship. *Competing* is a dimension related to whether there are winners and losers in the relationship versus a relationship typically resulting in mutual gain for both parties. *Economic exchange* refers to the personal advantage and/or detriment resulting from transactions that occur during the relationship. The continuum extends from great personal benefit to great personal sacrifice.

**Breadth** dimensions relate to how significant the relationship is. A relationship is more significant if it is broader in scope (spanning a lot of different interests and settings) and ongoing, or continuous. *Scope* refers to how far the relationship extends beyond narrow roles and limitations. Being someone's boss, mentor, and friend has more breadth than merely being that person's supervisor. *Time horizon* refers to whether the relationship is transactional and episodic versus continuous and ongoing.

**Affinity** dimensions concern the degree to which the people find each other intrinsically interesting. Affinity is strongest when individuals find each other stimulating, share things in common with each other, and are physically attracted to each other. *Stimulation* involves the amount of psychological energy the other person arouses in an individual. *Sharing things in common* relates to how much one is similar to another person. *Liking* is a positive emotional reaction to other people. *Romantic interest* is the degree of physical attraction another person has for an individual. (Note: Romantic interest is not a useful factor for considering relationships between groups.)

Uhl-Bien, Graen, and Scandura (2000) describe three levels of relationships that may occur, ranging from "low quality strangers" to "high-quality partners" (see Table 5.2). At the lowest level, **stranger** relationships are those characterized as contractually defined, formal exchanges based on limited trust and in-role interactions, lack of mutual respect, formal communications, little mutual understanding, limited support and commitment for one another, and no mutual obligation. In stranger relationships the individual participants are like interchangeable parts. At a moderate level, **acquaintance** relationships are those characterized as having increased social exchange and sharing of information and resources, contractual as well as limited noncontractual exchange, some trust, mutual respect and understanding, greater commitment, and some mutual obligation. And finally, at the highest level, **partnership** relationships are those characterized as involving teamwork based on respect, trust, and mutual obligation for one another, open communication with a sharing of inside information and resources, and commitment to one another and to the relationship.

Table 5.2 Levels of Relationship Quality

| Relationship Quality | Relationship Label | Relationship Characteristics |
|---|---|---|
| Low | Stranger | • Contractually defined |
| | | • Formal exchanges based on limited trust and in-role interactions |
| | | • Lack of mutual respect |
| | | • Formal communications |
| | | • Little mutual understanding |
| | | • Limited support and commitment for one another |
| | | • No mutual obligation |
| Medium | Acquaintance | • Increased social exchange and sharing of information and resources |
| | | • Contractual as well as limited noncontractual exchange |
| | | • Some trust, mutual respect, and understanding |
| | | • Greater commitment |
| | | • Some mutual obligation |

| High | Partnership | • Involving teamwork |
| | | • Based on respect, trust, and mutual obligation for one another |
| | | • Open communication with a sharing of inside information and resources |
| | | • Commitment to one another and the relationship |

Adapted from Uhl-Bien, Graen, & Scandura, 2000

It is important to realize that partnership relationships do not require symmetry. Brown and Eisenhardt (1998: 62–64) provide an instructive example from the Tour de France.

Behind each winner is a team because the Tour de France is both a team and an individual event. Team members can share sponsors, equipment, mechanics, tools, and training. Although the top member on the team is the one everyone knows, other team members are essential. They draft one another ... team members pace the race to play to one another's strengths and to mitigate weaknesses ... they muscle and block to protect teammates from passing moves by competitors ... and they do all of this in the context of one of the fastest-moving team sports on earth.

However, as they go on to explain, if there is no relationship beyond shared resources and sponsors, and team members compete for themselves, no one on the team can win, because no individual has the endurance to win as an individual. They also caution, team members should not collaborate equally, either. Individual differences must be recognized and accommodated or no individual member is likely to capture the yellow jersey of the winner, because no one on the team will be able to gain a sufficient advantage over the rest of the racing field. Effective partnerships require deliberate and insightful co-adaptation and management.

Relationships between people can be characterized as "strong" or "weak" ties. Strong ties are defined as those involving closeness, reciprocation, and substantial time spent with the other party; whereas weak ties are not close, there is less reciprocation, and the parties spend less time together (Granovetter, 1973). Individuals have networks of relationships that include both strong and weak ties.

Relationships with strong ties (for instance, partnerships, as described above) are not necessarily better than relationships with weak ties (for instance, acquaintances). In fact, a combination of both strong and weak relationships is necessary for effective organizational functioning. Ancona and Caldwell (2000) suggest that in configuring teams, it is best to have members who have connections with others both inside and outside of the organization. Since information and knowledge may be widely dispersed, team members with a wide range of different networks, both inside and outside of the organization, are most likely to bring needed information and knowledge to the group. Consequently, an effective team needs many weak ties. However, the team also needs strong ties between members and those outsiders who have access to, or control over, resources needed by the group. Lacking a strong tie, an outsider may be unwilling to expend the time necessary to obtain the needed resources.

Table 5.2    Levels of Relationship Quality

| Relationship Quality | Relationship Label | Relationship Characteristics |
| --- | --- | --- |
| Low | Stranger | • Contractually defined<br>• Formal exchanges based on limited trust and in-role interactions<br>• Lack of mutual respect<br>• Formal communications<br>• Little mutual understanding<br>• Limited support and commitment for one another<br>• No mutual obligation |
| Medium | Acquaintance | • Increased social exchange and sharing of information and resources<br>• Contractual as well as limited noncontractual exchange<br>• Some trust, mutual respect, and understanding<br>• Greater commitment<br>• Some mutual obligation |
| High | Partnership | • Involving teamwork<br>• Based on respect, trust, and mutual obligation for one another<br>• Open communication with a sharing of inside information and resources<br>• Commitment to one another and the relationship |

Adapted from Uhl-Bien, Graen, & Scandura, 2000

# Types of Relationships

There are six types of relationships that HR should actively manage (see Table 5.3). There are two categories of settings for each of these six relationships. One relationship category exists between parties that are both within the same organization (internal to internal). These internal-to-internal relationships are most often the traditional focus of HRM interventions. However, important relationships also exist between parties that cut across organizational boundaries. In this latter relationship category, one party is within the organization, whereas the other is outside of the organization (internal to external). These relationships are perhaps less familiar HRM territory, but they offer substantial potential for creating benefits throughout the value chain.

The first type of relationship (whether internal-to-internal or internal-to-external) is between two individuals (individual-individual). This type of relationship can occur between two individuals in the same organization (for instance, co-worker – co-worker or boss-subordinate). It also can occur between two individuals who are not members of the same organization (for instance, colleague-colleague). These types of relationships can be characterized as liking versus disliking; close versus distant; or strong versus weak. Through training and development activities, structured interactions, teambuilding, and similar activities, HRM can facilitate organizational efforts to make competitively important relationships move toward the high-liking and high-closeness ends of the spectrum in order to create stronger ties. Alternatively, HRM can facilitate organizational efforts to extend an individual's weak ties by encouraging participation in meetings, facilitating contacts within and outside of the organization, and so forth.

The second type of relationship is between an individual and a group (individual-group). This type of relationship can occur between an individual and a group within the same organization (for example, between an individual and a work group or department). It can also occur between an individual within an organization and a group outside of the organization (for example, between an individual and a neighborhood group as in neighborhood policing). These types of relationships can be characterized as in-group versus out-group. The relationship may be one of inclusion (being in the in-group) or exclusion (being in the out-group). Clearly, if HRM can assist employees to see customers, suppliers, and members of complementary firms as part of their in-group circle, these relationships are much more likely to yield competitively valuable interactions.

The third type of relationship is between an individual and an organization (individual-organization). This type of relationship can occur between an individual (that is, employee) and his or her organization (that is, employer). This is the traditional "employment relationship." It also can occur between an individual and an organization other than his or her employer (for instance, professional organization). These types of relationships can be characterized by loyalty and commitment versus transactional. Here the major change for HRM is to extend their efforts to foster loyalty and commitment to those beyond the boundaries of the organization. For example, the same kinds of techniques that HRM uses to help employees learn the ropes of the organization can be used to help new customers become attuned to organizational practices that will, in turn, enable them to deal more effectively and efficiently with the firm. Furthermore, organizations will have stronger ties with core employees than they will with temporary or part-time staff. The use of a combination of core and peripheral employees to benefit from both strong and weak ties resembles the strategy previously described by Ancona and Caldwell (2000).

The fourth type of relationship is between one group and another group (group-group). This type of relationship can occur between two groups in the same organization (for instance, engineering and marketing). It can also occur between two groups, one of which is within the organization and one of which is outside of the organization (for instance, an engineering group in one organization and an engineering group in another organization, such as a supplier). These types of relationships can be characterized as allies versus rivals. As organizations increasingly rely on relationships with other organizations to deal with complexity, capitalize on technology advances, and shape the marketplace, HRM's contribution to managing group dynamics needs to extend to groups comprising individuals that cut across organizational lines.

The fifth type of relationship is between a group and an organization (group-organization). Here, a group (for example, engineering) has a relationship with the larger organization of which it is a part. A union's relationship with an organization is another example. Or a group outside the firm (for example, Saturn customers) develops a relationship with the organization that sells the product they have in common. The relationship can be characterized as facilitative and contributing (versus obstructive). Differences in goals, time horizons, terminology, and similar contextual factors often make effective communication across groups quite challenging. Human resource management can offer a variety of interventions to ease the communication barriers among internal and external groups and thus make them more likely to contribute to mutually beneficial outcomes.

The sixth type of relationship is between organizations. These relationships can be characterized as involving strategic allies, complements, or archrivals. Often these relationships among firms change as the competitive landscape shifts. For example, competitors may form an alliance to create a new product application but still compete vigorously on the core products. Human resource management can help individuals and groups learn how to effectively navigate these complicated and delicate associations.

Relationships are a primary factor determining whether or not a complex social system is adaptive (Pascale, Milleman, & Gioja, 2000). Relationships are the basis for self-organization—the spontaneous reconfiguration of a system to respond effectively to emerging conditions. Reciprocal relationships are a requirement for self-organization to take place. As Pascale, Millemann, and Gioja (2000: 263) explain, "reciprocity provides the bonds that enable the distributed intelligence within a living system to cleave together for the common good. The stronger the linkages, the more capable the organism of adaptive work." In the knowledge economy, a firm's success depends on agile adaptability. Corporate leaders must rely on individuals within the firm to self-organize and design emergent strategies that move the firm forward without waiting for a long-term planning document to guide their decisions. Without effectively managed relationships, this strategic capability cannot be developed.

# Human Resource Management as Relationship Builder

The role of relationship builder both changes and extends the focus of traditional HRM. It changes the focus by directing attention to multiple relationships that create social capital and the capacity for self-organization in an organization. It extends the focus of HRM by directing attention not only to relationships within organizations but to those outside the walls of the firm, as well. Furthermore, the relationship builder role requires new activities, new methods, and new approaches that go beyond traditional HRM practices. The role of relationship builder involves six primary expectations (see Table 5.4).

First, as a relationship builder, HR must create opportunities for individuals to interact in such a way that they generate linkages that are strong, multidimensional, and reciprocal (Uhl-Bien, Graen, & Scandura, 2000) for creating the level of trust and sharing necessary to work together. However, HRM must also create opportunities for individuals to interact in a way that extends their information access through weak ties.

This means more than simply encouraging social interactions among employees. It requires creating conditions, nurturing motivation, and providing resources (Adler & Kwon, 2000). Uhl-Bien, Graen, and Scandura (2000) prescribe the "development of high quality dyadic relationships that stem out into strong relational networks within a culture that facilitates and rewards development of social capital through effective relationships." MacKenzie (1996) describes a meeting of Hallmark employees charged with developing a creative approach to the regional field meetings. The designated employees arrived in a room dominated by an overhead projector and proceeded to use the equipment, as intended, to display slide after slide of tables, charts, graphs, and similar data. Needless to say, little creativity or engagement resulted. But when MacKenzie, who became the facilitator, changed the environment by getting rid of the projector and introducing some candles, colored markers, and other artifacts for a very different kind of setting, those in the meeting let go of their corporate masks and became involved both in the task and with each other. The result was much more valuable and carried over to create a much more motivated field sales force. Human resource management needs to provide the "candles and crayons" that encourage people to reach out and connect.

Table 5.4 How Human Resource Management Can Build and Nurture Relationships

1. HRM can create opportunities for individuals to interact in such a way that they generate linkages that are strong, multidimensional, and reciprocal for creating the level of trust and sharing necessary to work together.

2. HRM can also create opportunities for individuals to interact in a way that extends their information access through weak ties.

3. HRM can map social capital ties that are relevant to the various tasks and challenges the organization faces and identify those that are strategically important.

4. HRM can be a source of support, advice, facilitation, and innovation for both formal and informal work groups, such as communities of practice.

5. HRM can develop ongoing, long-term relationships with former and current employees.

6. HRM can focus attention on how it can improve relationships across value-chain members (for example, suppliers, distributors, and customers).

There are numerous "high-tech" and "low-tech" approaches that can be used for creating conditions that encourage relationship building. These approaches can be used for nurturing both the strong and weak ties necessary for organizational effectiveness. Among the "high-tech" approaches, organizations are investing in collaborative technologies, such as shared knowledge repositories, chat rooms, and videoconferences (Cohen, 1997). For example, British Petroleum uses "virtual teamworking" that enables diverse individuals in different locations to develop richer relationships. Virtual teamworking stations are equipped with videoconferencing, multimedia e-mail, shared applications, a scanner, and an electronic whiteboard. Through the use of multiple media, individuals are able to see and hear people at their worksites, resulting in depth and context that is not available in less-rich media. This facilitates the creation of stronger ties that are more difficult to establish in "virtual teamworking."

By providing tools such as personal web pages, directories of expertise, and knowledge maps, individuals can locate others for whom they might have an affinity—creating an organizational "matchmaking" service. This facilitates the creation of weak ties that extend the network of individual members beyond their group boundaries. By enabling employees to access expertise quickly and easily through such weak ties, organizational processes can benefit.

Among the low-tech approaches, organizations are investing in architectural designs that promote interaction, as well as designing policies and procedures that stimulate discussions and communication (Cohen, 1997). These methods are similar to hanging a birdfeeder from a tree in your backyard and installing a birdbath in your garden. You can't force birds to interact at a specific location, but you can create an appealing environment that attracts them to do so. Likewise, in the workplace you can't force people to interact and establish relationships, but you can create conditions where those interactions will emerge.

For example, Opticon, a Danish firm, built stairwells in a new building with wide landings, a coffee machine, and a place to sit (Cohen & Prusak, 2001). This encourages employees to meet, have conversations, and develop relationships where these events occur, anyway. This approach is similar to building sidewalks on paths where people actually walk rather than where an architect wants to put them. Pitney Bowes Credit Corporation created a friendly workplace that encourages teamwork and communication (Cohen, 1997). Their new offices were designed to feel like a theme park: the carpet has a cobblestone pattern, there are faux gaslights, street signs, and a French-style café, where employees can gather. They also created a "cranial kitchen," where employees can surf the Web or watch training videos. Contrast Opticon's and Pitney Bowes' office designs with your local government office building (for instance, the drivers' license bureau) and you can quickly comprehend the importance of physical space design on encouraging and nurturing relationships.

Human resource management can become more actively involved in managing issues related to interaction, such as colocation, meetings, conferences, social events, employee roundtables, internal electronic communication networks, and other means for bringing people together. The pejorative past image of HRM as "plaid-coated picnic organizers" attempting to get people to work together as teammates in a sack race may be resurrected into a positive image of HRM as "relationship broker" using social skills to help individuals forge powerful and enduring business relationships. To some extent, this may mean making a part of everyday business life the informal, interpersonal experiences that have often been reserved for special occasions. For example, PIPSA, one of Mexico's leading paper manufacturers, encourages interdepartmental meetings wherein members often rely on the Mexican tradition of oral and musical storytelling to share their ideas (Matson, 1997). Rather than viewing organizationally sponsored social events as discretionary, they should instead be viewed as invaluable sources of relationship building.

In addition to simply creating conditions and hoping for relationships to develop, organizations can use formal hierarchies and roles, as well. By specifying work and decision flows, formal hierarchies can influence opportunities for relationships to develop. Many ties come with formal positions and are not voluntarily chosen, but these ties are not necessarily dysfunctional. Adler and Borys (1996) refer to "enabling" forms of bureaucracy (those which facilitate functional relationships) versus "coercive" ones in organizations. Bureaucracy does not have to result in stifled relationships. Enabling bureaucracies use rules, procedures, and formalization to help committed employees do their jobs more effectively and reinforce their commitment.

More traditional HRM activities—within the context of the formal organization—take on greater prominence from the relationship perspective. For example, orientation programs, socialization, mentoring programs, and job rotation are all potential means for fostering relationships. The role of HRM is to realize this potential and to leverage it for the organization's benefit. W.L. Gore Associates illustrates how strong interpersonal bonds can be developed through an effective mentoring program (Lussier & Achua, 2001). Their sponsor program joins an experienced, senior employee with a newly hired, inexperienced one. Before a candidate is hired, at least one senior employee has to agree to be a sponsor. The sponsor's responsibilities include: taking interest in the new employee's contributions, problems, and goals; coaching; and advocating for the new employee. The sponsor has a long-term commitment to the new employee. Over time, employees may have multiple sponsors. According to company documents, there are three types of sponsors: (1) a starting sponsor, who helps get the new employee started on the job or a current employee started on a new job, (2) an advocate sponsor, who sees to it that the employee gets credit and recognition for contributions and accomplishments, and (3) a compensation sponsor, who ensures that the employee receives fair rewards for contributions to the organization's success.

Viant, an Internet company, believes it takes about seven months to get new hires assimilated into the organization's culture (Cohen & Prusak, 2001). They require all employees to participate in a three-week orientation program that creates social connections that will help facilitate job performance long after the program is completed. The CEO calls himself the "chief cultural officer" and believes that this approach creates lasting bonds among employees and between employees and the organization. The company's 9% turnover rate (low for the industry) attests to his faith.

Second, as a relationship builder, HR must map social capital ties that are relevant to the various tasks and to the challenges the organization faces and identify those that are strategically important. Etienne Wenger recommends that organizations identify strategically important competencies and then search for communities that have that competence (Cohen & Prusak, 2001). This means, for example, interviewing known experts in those areas and determining whether they are part of a community (or if not, perhaps creating one). Human resource management must recognize and understand the various informal social relationships that are important, as well as the formal ones.

One important type of informal association of individuals in an organization—particularly important in a knowledge economy—is a **community of practice.** A community of practice is an informal cluster or network of people who work together sharing knowledge, solving problems, exchanging insights, stories, and frustrations (Lesser & Prusak, 2000). It is a group of people who exhibit all of the relationship dimensions described previously: rapport, bonding, breadth, and affinity. Communities of practice are not constrained by geographic, business unit, or functional boundaries. They are formed around common tasks, common work interests, and common contexts.

Many communities of practice may exist in an organization. These communities of practice are linked within the organization through complementary activities (Brown & Duguid, 2000). That is, different communities of practice complement one another in pursuit of the organization's objectives. For example, in a drug company, a community of practice that is formed around regulatory approval issues may be complemented by another community of practice formed around chemical delivery systems. Likewise, many communities of practice within an organization may be linked horizontally to other organizations through common or shared practices. These **networks of practice** (communities that extend beyond a single organization) extend relationships outside organization boundaries, bringing new knowledge and insight into the system. For example, Bristol-Meyers-Squibb found that their oncology division had been extremely successful for a long time, largely due to this group's rich networking outside of the organization's boundaries (Cohen & Prusak, 2001). The number of people both inside and outside this group's network was substantially larger than for any other division in the company. The task for HRM is to identify those communities of practice that have a direct impact on strategic objectives and invest in them (provide resources for face-to-face meetings, encourage cross-organizational communications, and so forth).

Third, as a relationship builder, HRM should be a source of support, advice, facilitation, and innovation for both formal and informal work groups, such as communities of practice. To do this effectively, HRM must dance between providing too much structure and influence (thereby stifling self-organization), and too little nurturance and attention and allowing problems to fester unnecessarily. To paraphrase Thomas Stewart (2000), organizations need to "water the grass, don't mow, and wait for lightning to strike." Informal relationships are like grass: They are low to the ground, they are easily mowed down, and they spread by dividing roots slowly to adjacent territory. Support, but not micromanagement, is necessary for nurturance. Too heavy an involvement and usurpation of the group may cause it to disband—to the detriment of the organization as well as the individuals. Wenger (2000) offers strategies to support communities of practice that could easily be extended to other types of informal groups in organizations:

- Have a sponsoring board of senior managers who give legitimacy to communities of practice and keep them in the loop
- Recognize participation in communities of practice through performance evaluations and promotion decisions
- Remove barriers such as counterproductive policies
- Provide budgets to cover such items as time, travel, and teleconferences

Fourth, as a relationship builder, HRM must monitor the organization to manage conflict and ensure that dysfunctional relationships and dysfunctional relationship networks are disbanded. At the individual level, dysfunctional relationships may evolve between supervisor and subordinate or between peers. Human resource management plays an important role in monitoring and intervening when problems between a supervisor and subordinate occur (a traditional role). It also plays an important supportive role for supervisors in managing conflict between peers.

At the group level, dysfunctional relationships may evolve within or between departments or other boundary conditions. Inbreeding, stagnation, and groupthink may occur in some cohesive groups. Here, HRM needs to intervene to introduce "functional" conflict in order to shake groups out of their negative inertia. In other cases of conflict between groups, HRM may need to intervene as a mediator or arbitrator in order to reduce "dysfunctional" conflict.

While informal groups and communities of practice can be a very positive influence on creating social capital within an organization, they can also be obstructive. For example, "old boy" networks (or social networks that exclude membership based on ethnicity or other non – job-related factors) limit the organizational benefits derived. Human resource management must be vigilant to ensure that informal groups are operating only in ways that benefit the organization and when necessary, disband groups that have goals that run counter to that of the organization.

Fifth, as a relationship builder, HRM must develop ongoing, long-term relationships with former employees, as well as current employees. One consulting firm runs outplacement programs for professional employees who voluntarily quit with the expectation that placements in other organizations might lead to additional business (Rousseau, 1998). Employees are socialized on the way out to develop a favorable impression of their former employer, thus creating loyal alumni. Deloitte and Touche rehires employees who have left at earlier stages in their careers. Termed "boomerang employees," their keeping-in-touch relationship strategy has a big payoff. Almost 15% of Deloitte and Touche's current employees are boomerangs (Rivera, 2001). David Reed of Accenture sums up the benefits of maintaining relationships with former employees. "Many leave to become our clients or they're hired by our clients, so we want to maintain goodwill with them."

Sixth, as a relationship builder, HRM must focus attention on how it can improve relationships across value-chain members (for instance, suppliers, distributors, and even customers). Relationships among value chain members include: relationships between people serving in liaison roles, relationships between groups that interact directly, and relationships between the top-management groups of the value chain partners (Greenhalgh, 2001). Value chain partners should also share HRM best practices to improve the efficiency and effectiveness of the whole value chain (Greenhalgh, 2001; Lengnick-Hall & Lengnick-Hall, 1999). Greenhalgh offers the following test to determine points of interaction: Think of the whole value chain as if it were vertically integrated within your own organization. What meetings, decisions, training programs, and so forth would the different partners participate in? We can add the following to Greenhalgh's question: How can HRM help facilitate this participation? For example, FedEx has developed technologies that increase connectivity and collaborative discussion within the company and a much closer relationship with their customers. Other companies have access to the operations of FedEx. Furthermore, FedEx can also enter some of their customers' operational areas. Old boundaries have been made porous for the benefit of all organizations involved.

# Conclusion

The creation of social capital that benefits an organization is a function of developing relationships between individuals, among groups, and across organizations. The combination of high-quality human capital and high-quality social capital is key to competitive advantage in the knowledge economy. High-quality relationships are those in which individuals, groups, or organizations work well together for mutual goals. In contrast, low-quality relationships are those in which individuals, groups, or organizations only do the minimum, or don't even get along well enough to work together.

Strong ties promote greater time and effort devoted to helping each other, whereas weak ties promote broader information access. In a world that is evermore connected (separated by only six people!), it is necessary for employees to have extensive relationship networks with both strong and weak ties. In the knowledge economy, HRM will need to nurture both human and social capital.

# Chapter 6

# Rapid Deployment Specialist

"Opportunity no longer knocks. These days, it darts past the door before you can even react."
—Anonymous advertisement

"We've gone from a world in which the big eat the small to a world in which the fast eat the slow."
—Thomas L. Freidman

The final role of the HR professional is to obtain the "right" human talent and ensure that people are in the right place, at the right time, able to perform the work that is needed, and able to achieve the desired outcomes: to rapidly deploy and redeploy human capital when and where it is needed. Although this responsibility is not a new one for HRM, the rapid pace and constantly changing market environment that many firms and industries confront has altered every element in the equation.

Some firms, such as those in the video game and movie industries, find that rather than creating and sustaining long-term competitive advantages that are nurtured and defended over time, success depends on their ability to create market disruptions and gain tactical advantages. This means relying on short-term, in-and-out, guerrilla-like tactics that allow them to take advantage of fleeting opportunities in the marketplace, while at the same time increasing the level of unpredictability for their rivals.

Other firms choose to be ephemeral by design. Some, like many biotechnology and medical device ventures, are formed to create new technologies or products. Often the expectation is that once their missions are accomplished, they will be absorbed by more powerful players. For these firms, effective HR deployment depends on flexibility and versatility. Others, like Nexus-Lexis, are virtual organizations whose network configurations change with the tides of the marketplace. For virtual firms, expediting the necessary HR depends on relationships and many loose ties (that is, informal, intermittent connections).

Still other firms, like Progressive Insurance, Albert Einstein Health Network, or Federal Express, realize that while the way they create value remains more stable, rapid response, agility, and short cycle times are powerful competitive weapons. For rapid response firms, the key drivers of performance are nimbleness, speed, and initiative.

In each of these scenarios, HRM needs to be able to rapidly assemble, concentrate, and deploy specific configurations of human capital to achieve precise strategic goals, and then be able to disassemble and redeploy this human talent as the situation changes. Strategic success depends on rapid, flexible, and opportunistic maneuvering through time and space.

How have the specific elements of effective HR deployment changed in the knowledge economy? First, *the firm's human talent* is likely to reach beyond its employees to include both customers and other individuals in the supply chain. Second, *the right place* is as likely to be in the field as it is on the production floor. Third, *the right time* is measured in minutes and hours rather than months or years. Having *the ability to perform the needed work* goes beyond knowledge, skills, and abilities for specific jobs to include more general competencies that enable adaptation to changing environmental demands. Finally, the knowledge economy demands personal commitment to, and accountability for, *outcomes* beyond an individual's direct control. The challenge for HR managers is enormous and begins with gaining a revised understanding of what it means to manage and effectively deploy a firm's human capital.

# Obtain the Right Human Talent

Traditionally, securing the human capital a firm needs involved recruiting, selecting, hiring, and training employees and then assigning those individuals to various jobs. This job-person match approach to HRM will constitute a much smaller proportion of the activities involved in securing the people necessary for a firm to accomplish its work in the knowledge economy for two reasons. First, the specific tasks and jobs to be performed are expected to be dynamic and to require continuous learning. Therefore, recruiting and selection activities will be focused on organization fit, value fit, and attitudes rather than hiring individuals with specific skills and experiences. Second, the knowledge economy increases the level of integration among activities along the entire supply chain. This means that suppliers and customers are often important contributors to the work of a firm. In this section we will discuss how "the right person" has been both redefined and extended.

## Redefining "The Right Person"

In the past, the "right person" for the job was the one who could perform the tasks specified in a job description. Expectations were that if applicants could perform the tasks in the job description, or if they had the ability to do so with some training, then they would be a good fit with the job. If the job changed dramatically over time, and employees could only perform what they were originally hired to do, they had to be replaced by new workers with new knowledge and skill sets.

The knowledge economy requires more from employees and their organizations. Task proficiency is still necessary, but it is no longer limited to the confines of a narrowly prescribed job description. In addition to having the knowledge and skills to perform a variety of tasks when needed, employees in the knowledge economy are also expected to quickly acquire new knowledge and skills that can be applied to new tasks when environmental or strategic conditions change.

Besides a broader array of task proficiency demanded of employees, the knowledge economy also places a premium on many important non – task-specific job behaviors. These other helping and productive behaviors have been defined as "contextual performance" (Borman & Motowidlo, 1993). Contextual performance includes behaviors such as the following.

- Persisting with enthusiasm and extra effort as necessary to complete one's own task activities successfully
- Volunteering to carry out task activities that are not formally part of one's own job
- Helping and cooperating with others
- Following organizational rules and procedures
- Endorsing, supporting, and defending organizational objectives
- Seeking out opportunities to contribute
- Anticipating problems or threats

Contextual performance is important for all jobs to varying degrees, however, it is even more important when organizations must rapidly assemble, concentrate, and deploy human talent, and then begin the process anew with little time to make adjustments. Organizations in the knowledge economy have little chance for survival if employees either *can't* or *won't* do something that needs to be done because "it's not in my job description." Employees must be willing and able to jump in where needed, take initiative, expend extra effort when required, and be willing to keep working under adverse conditions.

Rapid deployment of human talent requires employees who are flexible. Workers need to be adaptable, versatile, and tolerant of uncertainty to operate effectively in the constantly changing global market (Pulakos et al., 2000). The variety of conditions and situations to which workers will need to adapt is daunting: new people, new teams, novel and ill-defined problems, different cultures, new technology, challenging physical conditions, and so forth. Eight primary dimensions of adaptive performance have been identified and empirically tested (Pulakos et al., 2000).

- ***Handling emergencies or crisis situations:*** Reacting with appropriate and proper urgency in life-threatening, dangerous, or emergency situations; quickly analyzing options for dealing with danger or crises and their implications; making split second decisions based on clear and focused thinking; maintaining emotional control and objectivity while keeping focused on the situation at hand; stepping up to take action and handle danger or emergencies as necessary and appropriate

- *Handling work stress:* Remaining composed and cool when faced with difficult circumstances or a highly demanding workload/schedule; not overreacting to unexpected news or situations; managing frustration well by directing effort to constructive solutions rather than blaming others; demonstrating resilience and the highest levels of professionalism in stressful circumstances; acting as a calming and settling influence that others look to for guidance

- *Solving problems creatively:* Employing unique types of analyses and generating new, innovative ideas in complex areas; turning problems upside-down and inside-out to find fresh, new approaches; integrating seemingly unrelated information and developing creative solutions; entertaining wide ranging possibilities others may miss; thinking outside the given parameters to see if there is a more effective approach; developing innovative methods of obtaining or utilizing resources when insufficient resources are available to do the job

- **Dealing with uncertain/unpredictable work situations:** Taking effective action when necessary without having to know the total picture or having all the facts at hand; readily and easily changing gears in response to unpredictable or unexpected events and circumstances; effectively adjusting plans, goals, actions, or priorities to deal with changing situations; imposing structure for self and others that provide as much focus as possible in dynamic situations; not needing things to be black or white; refusing to be paralyzed by uncertainty or ambiguity

- **Learning work tasks, technologies, and procedures:** Demonstrating enthusiasm for learning new approaches and technologies for conducting work; doing what is necessary to keep knowledge and skills current; quickly and proficiently learning new methods or how to perform previously unlearned tasks; adjusting to new work processes and procedures; anticipating changes in the work demands and searching for and participating in assignments or training that will prepare oneself for these changes; taking action to improve work performance deficiencies

- **Demonstrating interpersonal adaptability:** Being flexible and open-minded when dealing with others; listening to and considering others' viewpoints and opinions and altering one's own opinion when it is appropriate to do so; being open and accepting of negative or developmental feedback regarding work; working well and developing effective relationships with highly diverse personalities; demonstrating keen insight of others' behavior and tailoring one's own behavior to persuade, influence, or work more effectively with them

- **Demonstrating cultural adaptability:** Taking action to learn about and understand the climate, orientation, needs, values, and so on of other groups, organizations, or cultures; integrating well into and being comfortable with different values, customs, and cultures; willingly adjusting behavior or appearance as necessary to comply with or show respect for others' values and customs; understanding the implications of one's actions and adjusting approach to maintain positive relationships with other groups, organizations, or cultures

- **Demonstrating physically oriented adaptability:** Adjusting to challenging environmental states such as extreme heat, humidity, cold, dirtiness, and so on; frequently pushing oneself physically to complete strenuous or demanding tasks; adjusting weight/muscular strength or becoming proficient in performing physical tasks as necessary for the job

The greater the range of adaptive performance behaviors that individuals possess, the better they will be able to adjust as knowledge economy organizations rapidly deploy and redeploy employees where they are best utilized.

In summary, the right person for the job in the knowledge economy is someone who has task proficiencies that are not confined to narrowly prescribed jobs. The right person is someone who facilitates peer and team performance by helping with job problems, being a good model, keeping the group goal-directed, and reinforcing participation by other group members (Campbell et al., 1993). And finally, the right person for the knowledge economy is adaptable and can confront new challenges and new obstacles with grace, a cool head, and sound judgment.

# Selecting the New Right Person for the Job

Obtaining employees in the knowledge economy requires new ways of viewing the selection process and new methods for assessing applicants. How do you hire employees who have a repertoire of skills, exhibit contextual performance, and are adaptable? If jobs are more temporary in duration (that is, more project-based, with the expectation that employees will be redeployed frequently), what knowledge, skills, abilities, and other characteristics of applicants do you assess in the selection process?

Firms as diverse as Nucor Steel, Southwest Airlines, Mitel Corporation, and Silicon Graphics have concluded that the right employees are not those with a particular set of skills or experiences; they are the individuals who blend initiative, team-spirit, and self-confidence with just the right values to fit their firm's particular approach to competitive success. Although factors such as integrity and a strong work ethic may be universal, many crucial values are firm-specific. Nucor, the innovative minimill, is concerned with screening for effective work habits in a dirty and dangerous environment. At Southwest Airlines, key values include humor and an unconventional perspective. Mitel Corporation, one of Canada's high-tech manufacturers, looks for comfort in challenging "sacred cows" and personal accountability. Silicon Graphics needs people who thrive in an autonomous and extremely informal environment.

Clearly, the particular attitudes and mind-sets being sought are unique to each firm, but four general principles appear to guide this culture-based approach to selection (Carbonara, 1996). First, finding the right person is based on the notion that while what you know and what you can do should change over time, who you are and what you value are more enduring. Culture-based selection assumes that basic personality traits do not change and that a fit between personal values and organizational values promotes success. A second principle is that, firms should be just as precise and deliberate in identifying and selecting for personal attributes as they have been in selecting for demonstrated skills and capabilities. Although culture-based selection focuses on "soft" issues, it should remain purposeful, specific, rigorous, disciplined, and strategy-oriented. Third, observed behaviors are more reliable indicators than self-report. Astute applicants are well-versed in the culture and personality of the company they hope will hire them. This can make it hard to rely on interview rhetoric to separate those who genuinely live certain values from those who are merely telling interviewers what they want to hear. Fourth, having the right applicant pool is a prerequisite for selecting the right candidates. Firms that rely on culture-based hiring tend to encourage referrals from current employees and other network-based hiring practices rather than rely on more traditional advertising and broad-based attraction approaches.

What is the role of the HR professional in putting these guidelines to work? Bowen, Ledford, and Nathan (1991) suggest a four-part process. These steps are summarized in Table 6.1. The first step is to conduct an assessment of the overall work environment including both job/work process analysis and organizational analysis to determine the behaviors and responsibilities that lead to overall effectiveness. But rather than focusing on specific tasks bundled into tight job descriptions, the focus is on work processes whereby task assignments can be fluid and tailored to meet temporal needs. In this step, HRM must determine the role an individual is expected to play within a stream of organization activities. A crucial factor that often has been overlooked is the contribution human capital is expected to make to strategy formulation and implementation (Dyer, 1984; Lengnick-Hall & Lengnick-Hall, 1988). The resource-based view of strategy (for example, Barney, 1995) provides a compelling argument that a firm's human capital offers the kind of rare, valuable, inimitable, and exploitable resource base that is an effective foundation for a firm's competitive strategy development.

Next, the type of person the firm requires needs to be determined. This includes an assessment of technical knowledge, skills, and abilities; social skills; personal needs, values and interests; and personality traits. Balancing the requirements of current performance against the expectations for future adaptability ensures that work context, as well as work content, is considered. People are hired for who they are, not just for what they can do. An organization-fit approach to staffing emphasizes the long-term strategic value an individual is expected to contribute to the firm (Snow & Snell, 1993). If firms are to have a diverse and flexible array of strategic moves available to enact, they must maintain an equally diverse and versatile intellectual capital repertoire (Volberta, 1996). Human resource management must therefore design innovative systems that select and develop individuals who learn and adapt quickly to new situations and can provide a firm with competitive flexibility and agility.

Table 6.1 Steps for Selecting the New Right Person for the Job

| Selection Step | Questions To Ask |
| --- | --- |
| • Conduct an assessment of the overall work environment, including both work process analysis and organizational analysis, to determine the behaviors and responsibilities that lead to overall effectiveness. | • What role(s) will individuals play in the organization? |
| | • What are the current and future needs of the organization? |
| | • How are environmental forces likely to change in the future (technology, markets, etc.)? |
| • Determine the type of person the firm needs. | • What technical knowledge, skills, and abilities does the firm need now and in the future? |
| | • How can contextual performance and adaptability be assessed? |
| | • What personality traits fit with the organization's culture? |

• Design "rites of passage" that enable both the firm and the individual to assess fit.

• Create multiple systems to reinforce the crucial values and behaviors.

• What personal values and attitudes fit with the organization's culture?

• How can the organization present its important cultural values and norms to applicants?

• What selection process features can be designed to provide applicants with a realistic preview of the organization?

• What selection process features can be designed to provide the organization with a realistic preview of the applicant?

• What values and behaviors are desirable to reinforce?

• How can desired values and behaviors be reinforced through appraisal, compensation, and training systems?

• What organizational rituals can be used to reinforce desired values and behaviors?

The third step is to design "rites of passage" that enable both the firm and the individual to assess fit. This includes the use of multiple screening devices, raters, and criteria during the selection process. Effective firms are relying on a variety of rigorous and reliable ways to assess the desired traits including simulations, in-box exercises, work trials, situational interviews, work activities, and observations of work behaviors in a number of settings. The result is a process that identifies individuals with the desired profile and provides a realistic preview of the workplace so that applicants can assess their own compatibility. These extensive selection processes ensure that successful candidates feel a sense of accomplishment once they are hired.

The final step in enabling person-organization fit is to create multiple systems to reinforce the crucial values and behaviors. For example, in high-involvement firms, a skill-based or competency-based pay system typically is used to reward employees for enhancing their ability to contribute to the firm. Similarly, if employees are responsible for decision making, it is essential that the information system is user-friendly and up-to-date. Skilled employees can be motivated to make effective discretionary decisions through the use of appropriate appraisal and compensation systems (MacDuffie, 1995). Likewise, frequent training opportunities can both increase the available skill repertoire for the firm and send a clear signal that continuous learning is expected (Wright & Snell, 1998). Rituals that identify and celebrate model behaviors, such as Herb Kelleher's unconventional annual meetings with employees at Southwest Airlines or Mitel's "Demo Days"—internal trade shows of innovative ideas—reinforce the essence of a firm's culture in vivid and memorable ways. This last step integrates selection with other HRM activities and with the firm as a whole.

# The Right Person May Be Outside of the Organization

Both suppliers and customers have the potential for making direct and important contributions to a firm's activities and competitiveness. The boundary between the organization producing the goods and services and the individuals and firms that constitute the extended value chain is increasingly permeable. As a result, individuals at various points along the transformation process, from raw materials to purchased goods, can be considered an integral part of the HR pool for an organization (Mills, Chase, & Margulies, 1983; Lengnick-Hall, 1996; Lengnick-Hall & Lengnick-Hall, 1999). For example, customers can be invaluable resources for creating an attractive ambiance that encourages repeat business in a restaurant. Chaparral Steel's customers provide the venue for field tests and experimentation with new products. Computer firms have Web sites and technicians that enable customers to reconfigure, repair, and debug the products they buy. Aircraft manufacturers use ERP systems that initiate production runs within their parts suppliers' factories. The list of ways in which suppliers, customers, and strategic partners contribute directly to an organization's productive capabilities grows daily. The most common term for this is *co-production*.

**Co-production** means that individuals beyond the borders of the firm collaborate with employees and contribute directly to the organization's work (Bowen, 1986). Co-production goes beyond traditional notions of customer responsiveness or accommodation. In a co-production relationship, customers or suppliers work directly with the firm's employees to make value-added contributions to increased productivity. For co-production to be effective, customers or suppliers must understand the work processes, must know what to do, must have the ability to perform the necessary tasks, and must be motivated to perform effectively and efficiently. The new HR professional, therefore, must be able to facilitate co-production and enable individuals external to the firm to behave as quasi employees. Rapidly assembling, concentrating, and deploying human talent includes these quasi employees along with regular employees.

Progressive Insurance, for example, recognizes that there is a learning curve for their clients associated with getting the most from what the company provides. For their immediate response strategy to be put into action, a client must call the firm to report an accident. The quicker the report is made, the greater the benefits from the rapid and seamless integration of people and technology that Progressive has orchestrated to process claims. Their company goal is to have every accident reported within 24 hours. An important question for the company, then, is how to encourage clients to make an immediate report of any accident. Human resource management activities such as performance assessment, job-enabling devices, and integrated work design provide the foundation for shaping desired customer behaviors. Thus, one part of the answer was developing a metric called the Claims Reporting Index, which monitors how long it takes customers to report an accident. Another element was designing a plastic card that looks like a credit card and contains the firm's toll-free claims number, the policy number, and other pertinent information. The card can be easily broken in half to make information exchange after an accident simple and relatively error-proof. A third ingredient is a sophisticated triage system of call centers that link field representatives, the company's mainframe data and systems, dispatchers, and others involved in resolving the claim. The triage system provides a transparent and uninterrupted flow of information between the customer, Progressive's central database, and the local claims activities.

Progressive's HR managers are able to contribute to each of these elements and to create an effective climate for action. As with internal employees, co-producers need clear and familiar work guidelines to learn about specific roles, boundaries, actions, and avenues for performing the needed tasks. Developing ideas for informing clients about the need for speedy reporting is analogous to employee orientation. As Bowen (1986) points out, external "employees" require both place orientation to help them figure out the setting and functional orientation to help them understand how the firm operates. Providing customers with easy and convenient tools for effective action, such as the plastic cards containing key information, is similar to ensuring that employees have the necessary information, technology, and other resources to do their jobs effectively. Human resource management needs to use its knowledge of human behavior to ensure that external employees can quickly and accurately decipher organizational signals.

The more other members of the supply chain are expected to coproduce, the more important it is to ensure that relevant organizational policies and practices become embedded in the materials the firm distributes to its external audience. Helping customers understand and appreciate the personal benefits of accurate and swift accident reports parallels the need to motivate employees to behave in certain ways to enhance organizational productivity and their own rewards. The basic goals are familiar HR objectives, but the target audience is quite different.

**Factors contributing to increased co-production.** As products and services are increasingly bundled, co-production becomes mandatory for many organizations. Co-production is essential when service production and delivery are inseparable, as is the case in education, health care, or any human service operation. The need for co-production increases as work becomes increasingly complicated, creating interdependencies between providers and customers and requiring greater amounts of knowledge exchange. Consulting firms that facilitate the implementation of complicated information technologies, for example, must partner with the organizations that hire them if the resulting systems are to work effectively. Research has found that inter-organizational project teams that blend employees from multiple firms yield the best performance in these situations (Crampton, 2000).

Co-production is particularly important when the boundaries between suppliers, producers, and customers become blurred. As Internet and similar information technologies increasingly link the production and operations of firms throughout the supply chain, employees in these organizations must be able to collaborate across organizational borders to ensure seamless transformations. As we move toward a more knowledge-based economy, the intangibility of desired outcomes nearly mandates increased co-production so that processes can be negotiated and results evaluated in real time. Human resource management professionals can contribute to organizational effectiveness by applying their knowledge of group dynamics, stewardship, agency theory (a theory of motivation that depicts exchange relationships between two parties), volunteerism, and other aspects of organization behavior to facilitate co-production.

The potential benefits of effectively managed co-production are enormous. Schneider and Bowen (1995) identified a number of possible advantages resulting from co-production, such as productivity increases that result in lower prices, shorter waiting times, and greater customization. These outcomes are not only beneficial for customers but also are likely to lead to stronger relationships between customers and the firms producing goods and services leading to increased customer loyalty and self-imposed switching costs. As a result, if HRM is able to increase a firm's capability for, or effectiveness at, managing co-production, then it can make several substantial contributions to the firm's sources of competitive advantage.

**Human resource management contributions to co-production effectiveness.** The need for co-production introduces several new elements for HR managers (see Table 6.2). First, HR must be able to effectively manage both physical and psychological borders and boundaries in new ways. The roles that customers or suppliers assume in organization activities should be explicitly defined. It needs to be clear whether the external contributor is considered a team member, resource person, evaluator, or technical expert. In addition, the co-producer's particular contribution to work processes needs to be clearly defined. Human resource management can contribute to effective co-production by creating work descriptions and role designations for various individuals external to the firm that parallel those created for employees. The co-producer's place in space also needs to be designated. For example, will co-production take place on organizational sites, in cyberspace, or in the field? Human resource management's role in managing external contributors will vary depending on whether co-production takes place face-to-face or through technology, and whether it is on-site or off-site. Finally, it will be important for HRM to create psychological ownership of processes and outcomes among external contributors that mirrors levels of commitment and involvement on the part of internal employees. Often this means sharing results and performance outcomes directly with external contributors and internal employees.

Second, HR can assist in managing important co-production relationships by clarifying important role distinctions. Research has shown that co-production is not as effective if internal employees "go native" and begin to identify more with the customers or suppliers than with their own firm (Crampton, 2000). Three relationships must be managed: the links between the production or service delivery employees and the customer; the connection between the organization and the customer; and the ties between the organization and the production or service delivery employee. Maintaining the necessary balance and distinctions between these links will be a significant HRM responsibility.

Table 6.2 Co-production: Managing Human Resources Outside of the Organization

| HR Responsibility | HR Actions |
| --- | --- |
| Manage physical and psychological borders of the organization. | • Define roles that customers, suppliers, and others will assume in organizational activities (team member, resource person, evaluator, or technical expert). |
| | • Create job descriptions and role designations for various individuals external to the firm that parallel those created for employees. |
| | • Determine where co-production will take place: face-to-face or through technology, and on-site or off-site. |
| | • Create psychological ownership of processes and outcomes among co-producers by sharing relevant information with them. |
| Clarify important role distinctions. | • Clarify role distinctions between the production or service delivery employees and the customer. |
| | • Clarify role distinctions between the organization and the customer. |

| | |
|---|---|
| | • Clarify role distinctions between the organization and the production or service delivery employees. |
| Develop organization's co-production capabilities. | • Adapt teambuilding to include those outside of the organization. |
| | • Assign responsibilities to those outside of the organization. |
| | • Develop facilitative communication structures such as communication cues and signage. |
| | • Socialize those outside of the organization (that is, orientation for co-producers). |
| Create new human capital capabilities. | • Nurture a climate of reciprocal trust between employees and co-producers. |
| | • Foster a long-term focus on interdependence between internal and external members of the workforce. |
| Manage co-producers as volunteer employees. | • Assess the consequences of continuous versus intermittent relationships with co-producers. |
| | • Develop creative ways to discipline co-producers without resulting in negative consequences for the organization. |

Third, HRM professionals will be primarily responsible for ensuring that organizations develop co-production capabilities. Both competence at managing relationships across the firm's boundaries and concern with external stakeholders are necessary. Co-production capabilities will require new approaches to activities such as teambuilding, assigning responsibility, and designing facilitative structures such as communication cues and signage. Organizations will also socialize co-producers, much as they do new employees (for instance, via orientation programs). Health clubs that offer a few free hours with a personal trainer are an example of organizations that recognize and respond to the need to socialize an expanded audience.

Fourth, new human capital capabilities will need to be developed within the workforce. Human resource management can contribute to creating an organization climate among both employees and co-producers that leads to reciprocal trust. Recent research (for example, Shafer et al., 2001) suggests that a context for action built upon core values that are known, understood, shared, and actively lived, provides a necessary foundation for trust and personal accountability. Both internal and external members of the workforce will need to internalize the importance of managing for long-term interdependence rather than focusing solely on the immediate transaction. In many ways this reflects the type of HRM role changes discussed in the chapter on stewardship.

Important differences must be recognized in the opportunities for selection and training of suppliers or customers versus selection and training of internal employees. It is unlikely, and in many instances (for example, insurance claims, health problems) undesirable, to maintain continuous contact with customers. This means that both training and behavioral consequences generally are intermittent, making both learning and behavioral change more difficult. In addition, "firing" a poorly performing customer directly alters demand for a product or service in a way that is quite different from terminating an unproductive employee. The range of options available for dealing with lack of compliance is much more restricted with co-production than with in-house activities. Moreover, there is little to prevent customers from abdicating their role as co-producer if they do not recognize or value the potential benefits. Some customers prefer total discretion in how they interact with business organizations. As a result of these factors, HR professionals will need to develop versatile and creative approaches to managing the firm's external human resources that reflect a clear understanding that this is a voluntary work force. When co-producers (be they customers, suppliers, or distributors, and so on) are effectively managed, they add a potent capacity that enables and extends the rapid deployment of human talent for the firm's purposes.

# Be in the Right Place

Two factors are redefining the right place for work to be done in the knowledge economy. First, the clear distinction between products and services is eroding. Product firms often attempt to ward off commoditization (a process in which products and services lose their distinctiveness so that competition becomes increasingly intense and focused almost exclusively on price) by wrapping their products in services intended to create a relationship with their customers. For example, computer manufacturers surround their products with services such as diagnostic help and build-to-order designs that encourage customer-organization ties. At the same time, service organizations, such as information technology consultants, are beginning to offer spreadsheets, workbooks, performance appraisal templates, and similar tangible products in an effort to make their contribution more concrete and thus more easily distinguished from that of competitors. This integration of products and services puts a premium on being able to work closely with customers and understand the precise conditions under which an organization's outputs will be used. Therefore organizational work often moves beyond organizational boundaries.

A second factor changing the right place is the development of sophisticated information technology. Advanced technologies are eliminating the need for people to be located in the same physical space to work together. With today's technology, the right place can be a virtual location in cyberspace. Consequently much of our understanding of group dynamics, team-building processes, and communication networks will need to be modified to reflect this emerging way of working together across broad distances.

Together, these factors are mobilizing the workplace and redefining location from physical space to psychological space. Having human resources at the right place in the knowledge economy means reconsidering what is meant by location, orchestrating team members who are physically distant, and creating a group effort that crosses traditional organizational, discipline, and physical boundaries. Ensuring that human resources are in the right place is an outcome of effective concentration.

**Concentration** is defined as the deliberate convergence and focus of effort and resources at the crucial time and space (Hamel & Prahalad, 1993; U.S. Marine Corps, 1989). The benefits of effective concentration should not be underestimated. Concentration enables resources to be applied for maximum benefit. Concentration of resources can result in decisive local superiority for organizations that have overall resource-inferiority. A combination of speed and concentration creates powerful momentum for shaping the marketplace. However, it is important to recognize that concentration requires accepting the risks associated with heightened vulnerability at alternate times and other places. Three factors lead to effective resource concentration: uncompromising focus, decisive timing, and precise positioning. Mobilizing the workplace and redefining place in a way that reflects the reality of knowledge-based competition are essential capabilities that contribute to a firm's ability for successful timing and positioning.

## Mobilizing the Workplace

As customization and co-production become more prevalent, it becomes increasingly difficult to respond to local situations if the workplace remains fixed within the walls of a factory or corporate office. Technology advances enable people to telecommute or take their work on the road. In the knowledge economy, work needs to become portable, and this means developing a number of new skills within the workforce and new design mechanisms within the firm.

When work takes place within an office, factory, or service center, a number of social, architectural, and mechanical factors create order and a structure for jobs. Hierarchical reporting relationships and interactions with co-workers define boundaries of behavior and provide easily observed performance norms. Office clusters, building configurations, plant layouts, and other architectural features provide natural boundaries to work flows and communication patterns. Machines and logistics help establish work pacing. When these familiar sources of order are removed by transporting work to a field setting or to the home, people need to be able to develop their own mechanisms to structure the workday and work activities. Human resource management can play an important role in developing the needed personal capabilities and in providing useful organizational mechanisms and tools. One of the most important personal skills for HRM to develop among the workforce is self-management—a set of both behavioral and cognitive strategies a person uses to influence and improve his or her own behavior (Manz & Sims, 1980).

Structural mechanisms are equally important in facilitating work mobilization (see Table 6.3). One of the most useful is a portable architecture or hierarchy. Military special forces units, for example, are able to achieve exceptional mobility, mission-specific flexibility, and speed by relying on four structural devices: rank, personal reciprocal interdependence, appropriate distance, and molecularization.

The overlay of military rank designates a specific and a relative place in the official pecking order for each individual. Rank denotes a position, a role, and a series of task responsibilities that are designated independently of a particular group assignment. Teams are designed with deliberate redundancy embedded in team composition so the overlay of rank quickly establishes order despite fluid team membership. Rank enables a kaleidoscope of skills, personalities, experiences, and assignments to be quickly orchestrated at any point in time. The rank structure makes it clear who is in charge in a highly flexible and deliberately uncongealed organization setting. Therefore, one way that HRM can contribute to effective rapid HR deployment is to design firm-specific means to establish personal hierarchical position. While this notion may run counter to some currently popular concepts such as empowerment, self-managed teams, and reduced status differences (for example, Pfeffer & Veiga, 1999), it is consistent with research on participative decision making that prescribes more autocratic decision making methods when time is limited (Vroom & Jago, 1988).

Table 6.3 Mobilizing the Workforce

| Mobilizing Principle | Definition | HR Practices |
|---|---|---|
| Establish a portable hierarchy. | • Rank denotes a position, a role, and a series of task responsibilities that are designated independently of a particular group assignment. | Design firm-specific means to establish personal hierarchical position. |

• Teams are designed with deliberate redundancy embedded in team composition so the overlay of rank quickly establishes order despite fluid team membership.

Create personal reciprocal interdependence.

• A compelling incentive for all involved to work together is needed to accomplish missions and develop desirable external images despite interpersonal conflicts or lack of familiarity from short time spent together as a team.

Design and implement assignment and performance appraisal practices that foster personal reciprocal interdependence across people, teams, and hierarchical levels.

Maintain appropriate distance between hierarchical levels.

• Role distinctions make rapid deployment and re-deployment easier

Organization norms, fluid assignments, socialization approaches and similar workplace value-creating practices can reinforce both the importance of many loose ties within the firm and the need for commitment to the firm over more parochial loyalties.

• Group cohesion is established for the larger organization, not specific units within it.

| Use molecularization. | • Individuals or groups form the basis for developing clusters that are formed and re-formed as needed. | Foster both the intellectual capital and the structural bonds that make organizational molecularization possible. |
|---|---|---|

Personal reciprocal interdependence across the hierarchy is a second crucial linking device that comes from military special forces units. Career success of the team captain (an officer) and the team sergeant (the top ranking NCO), for example, are intimately intertwined (Simons, 1997). The reputation of the captain among other officers in the organizational hierarchy (for example, battalion and group commanders) has a great deal to do with the desirability of assignments a team receives. This provides a strong incentive for the team sergeant and other team members to promote and cultivate a strong positive image of their team captain throughout the company. Likewise, a team captain is dependent on his team to provide crucial opportunities for him to accomplish objectives that are essential to his own future career path (for example, learn field craft, hone leadership and decision-making skills, gain a desirable reputation within the chain of command). Personal reciprocal interdependence provides a compelling incentive for all involved to work together to accomplish missions and develop desirable external images despite interpersonal conflicts or lack of familiarity from short tenure as a team. This suggests that another way in which HRM can contribute to effective rapid HR deployment is to design and implement assignment and performance appraisal practices that foster personal reciprocal interdependence across people, teams, and hierarchical levels.

A third mechanism influencing effective resource deployment that emerges from special forces operations is the concept of appropriate distance. Both formal regulations and informal norms dictate ways in which officers should maintain distance from their men and in which senior NCOs should distance themselves from more junior soldiers (Simons, 1997). Loose ties contribute to flexibility, enabling units to be assembled, disbanded, and reassembled as missions require without regard to personal relationships. In addition, loose ties reinforce the idea that while commitment and trust within a team and among team members is essential, commitment and trust within the larger special forces branch is paramount. This suggests a third way in which HRM can contribute to effective rapid HR deployment. Organizational norms, fluid assignments, socialization approaches, and similar workplace value-creating practices can reinforce both the importance of many loose ties within the firm and the need for commitment to the firm over more parochial loyalties.

Finally, making the right place portable often relies on molecularization. Tapscott (1995) argues that the knowledge economy is a molecular economy in which "mass" becomes "modular." The term *molecularization* reflects concepts drawn from physics. A molecule is the smallest particle into which a substance can be divided and still retain the chemical properties of the original substance. In the knowledge economy, organization molecules can be individual knowledge workers who create value independently or they can be fluid work units or cells that collaborate to accomplish a mission. To the extent the workforce is motivated, self-learning, disciplined, and entrepreneurial, molecular clusters can be formed and disbanded as conditions require. As a result, place can be continuously redefined to reflect competitive conditions and productivity needs. Human resource management will need to foster both the intellectual capital and the structural bonds that make organizational molecularization possible.

Molecularization is often triggered by growth and the need to make successful operations scaleable. There are a number of important ways that HRM can help a firm build-to-scale. One of the most important is by creating a detailed map of who does what, who reports to whom, and what metrics affect each employee's compensation. A map of this kind helps ensure that each current and future employee is contributing to the company-wide goals that create strategic success. Attention to details is a key element that keeps employees aligned when growth and change are the norm (Salter, 2000). Human resource management can also make value-added contributions to scaleability by developing sufficiently rich orientation and knowledge management programs that employees are able to create and maintain a strong sense of community and personal connections, even as numbers swell.

Through a combination of self-management, portable hierarchy, interdependence, loose ties, and molecularization, HRM can design the personal capabilities and structural links that create self-sufficient teams that are able to complete assignments with a great deal of disciplined operational autonomy. At the same time, these human and structural capabilities provide a basis for strategic governance that is centralized, formal, and exceptionally productive when rapid deployment is essential.

# Replacing Physical Place with Psychological Place

Reconceptualizing place to mean working together on a common issue rather than working in the same room enables HRM to rethink the ways in which location can allow people to contribute to a firm's competitive advantage. For example, Global Knowledge Services provides strategic information to clients around the globe. Often the need for data is immediate. Rather than hiring people who are willing to work around the clock, they have hired a network of researchers on the east and west coasts of the United States and in the Philippines who use the Internet to cross geographic and timeline boundaries. This enables the firm to provide service 24/7 without requiring its HR to work extraordinary hours.

To transform physical location into psychological location, individuals with very different perspectives must be able to interpret and use many types of information effectively and toward a common purpose. Employees, and many who are external to a firm, will have direct access to real time information at multiple locations within a firm and in the field. Information transparency is a prerequisite for effective decentralized and autonomous decision making. For information to be transparent, not only does data need to be accessible in many locations, people need to know how to transform data that may be generated outside their sphere of expertise into effective choices and actions. This requires enterprise-based training and a clear understanding of organizational goals and metrics.

A very dispersed workforce also means that a strong culture and a common passion, rather than rules or supervision, must provide the guidance system for autonomous choices and behaviors. Rosenbluth International takes this very seriously and has initiated countless culture-building practices that transform the typical rhetoric into a vital reality in its widely separated offices. New employees are presented with a "goodies bag" that includes lunch coupons, cheat-sheets to introduce co-workers, office supplies, and similar gifts that make it easier to develop relationships within the firm and provide tangible reminders that the firm is glad the new employee is on board. Managers and subordinates switch roles periodically to ensure that individuals understand the consequences of their choices on other employees up and down the hierarchy. Periodic contests, movie days, and similar events regularly reinforce values, relationships, and team spirit messages. The result is a firm that capitalizes on flexibility by providing a common thread that runs throughout its diverse and geographically far-flung units.

## Act at the Right Time

In the high-velocity knowledge economy, speed is a prerequisite for gaining an economic payback from technology and innovation (Matson, 1996; Eisenhardt & Tabrizi, 1995). As Fine (1998) explains, the clockspeed, or evolutionary life cycle, of many industries is accelerating, meaning that more and more competition revolves around achieving temporary advantage. Industries from personal computers to entertainment are finding that two-year development cycles are ineffective in industries governed by supply chains that shift weekly or monthly.

Quick response is also a direct source of competitive advantage. From quick turnaround times for aircraft to rapid response on insurance claims to immediate commercialization of movie tie-ins, there are ample illustrations that the ability to move quickly leads to greater resource utilization and lower costs. The ability to fix a problem on the spot, authorize an immediate exchange for a damaged product, or execute a stock transaction in a nanosecond demonstrates a firm's responsiveness to customer needs and leads to consumer loyalty.

Speed can improve accuracy. When an adverse drug reaction is detected immediately or when a claims agent can observe an accident scene before vehicles have been moved, the root source of a problem is easier to detect and fix, and it is less likely that a firm will respond to secondary symptoms.

Speed can enable a firm to adjust its pace to meet market conditions. As firms move toward just-in-time production, all of those organizations along their supply chain must be able to adjust their processing speed to match that of the dominant player. As product customization becomes the industry standard, firms with quick development and production cycles will outperform those with slower internal responses. Many firms are just beginning to recognize the value of speed as an important competitive resource.

Speed is the ability to move and change rapidly. In hypercompetitive environments (that is, those that change rapidly, relentlessly, and discontinuously), firms must be able to move in new directions before their rivals and turn on a dime to capitalize on new opportunities (D'Aveni, 1994). To achieve advantages from speed, firms must be able to increase their agility and quickness without sacrificing quality or raising costs (Dyer & Shafer, 1999).

Zara, Spain's global fashion retailer, is a good example of a firm that capitalizes on speed. The company relies on intelligence gathering, technology links, an integrated supply chain, and coordination to redefine the clothing trade with just-in-time, low-cost fashion. Since Zara takes only four to five weeks to design a new collection and less than a week to produce it, the firm can spot a fashion trend or a music video and have it available for sale in little more than a month. Competitors like Benetton often require nine months to complete the same cycle.

Human resource management can contribute to a firm's response speed in a number of ways: creating triage capabilities, integrating technology and people, creating small wins, and developing resourceful employees (see Table 6.4).

Table 6.4 How Human Resources Can Contribute to Rapid Responsiveness

| Strategy | Methods |
|---|---|
| Create triage capabilities. | • Develop, compile, and maintain information on a firm's HR capabilities. |
| | • Use information technology to identify and deploy HR quickly. |
| | • Help individuals design appropriate personal performance metrics that link their contributions to organizational goals and strategies. |
| Integrate technology and people. | • Fit technology to the situation and employees rather than vice versa. |
| | • Assess opportunities for low-tech/high-tech combinations that provide desired speed. |
| Create small wins. | • Subdivide large-scale organizational objectives into smaller ones. |
| | • Identify individual goals that fit with overall organization change objectives. |
| Develop employee resourcefulness. | • Allow employees to work on personally important, enriched, and meaningful tasks. |
| | • Allow employees freedom to choose how they carry out their work. |
| | • Create a mutually supportive work group climate. |

- Develop supervisors that lead but don't micromanage.

- Ensure that top management visibly supports resourceful behavior.

- Remove organizational impediments to creative processes.

# Creating Triage Capabilities

Triage is a concept of sorting and choosing that concentrates scarce resources where they will have the most benefit. The first organizational use was to allocate medical assistance so that care would be given first to those who would survive only with immediate help. This prevented misallocation of scarce resources to those who would recover without treatment or who were too severely wounded to survive regardless of care. In business organizations, an effective triage system is essential for allocating scarce human talent quickly to where skills and abilities will create the greatest value.

Human resource management can contribute to creating effective HR triage systems in two ways. First, HRM is instrumental in developing, compiling, and maintaining information on a firm's HR capabilities. Maintaining a thorough and current HR information system (HRIS) is crucial for knowing who's qualified and who's available for a particular need at a specific point in time.

Netigy, an up-and-coming e-commerce services provider, understands this well. When account executives contract with clients for a job, they can immediately access the company's HRIS to find the necessary human capital to complete the assignment. The system contains everything they need to know from the consultants' technical certifications to their prior experience to current commitments to travel preferences. The system also evaluates each consultant based on specific qualifications so that managers can easily distinguish among potential candidates for the job. The system allows executives to decide to substitute one consultant for another on an existing assignment if they need to free up an expert with unique abilities.

Human resource management also contributes to effective triage systems by helping individuals design appropriate personal performance metrics that link their contributions to organizational goals and strategies. In some cases personal metrics can be derived from strategy. Kaplan and Norton (2001), for example, explain how some strategically focused firms have created small, fold-up, personal scorecards for each of their employees. Each card contains information on corporate objectives and measures, business unit translations of the corporate goals into its own specific performance drivers, and personal performance objectives and near-term action steps needed to achieve these goals. Personal metric systems aid in effective triage by enabling employees who are geographically dispersed to make autonomous decisions and take independent actions but ensure that they understand how their choices contribute to important organizational objectives.

By maintaining an HRIS that is updated in real time, organizations can quickly identify human talent that can be deployed rapidly. By integrating technology with people, organizations enhance the capabilities of human capital to respond rapidly. Finally, by developing personal metric systems, organizations can rapidly coordinate the individual efforts of employees who may be geographically dispersed.

## Integrating Technology and People

As discussed in the chapter on HRM's knowledge facilitation role, there are substantial connections between information technologies and a firm's intellectual capital. Information technology is also an important enabler of speed, but the choice of technology solution needs to fit the situational requirements. This is where HRM can make a significant contribution.

Some settings, such as Toyota's use of the Internet to create a sense of community, collaboration, and loyalty within the firm and across the supply chain, requires very sophisticated information technology solutions based on high-level hardware and software. Other situations, such as Zap Courier's bike messenger service, requires a different mix. Zap couples sophisticated software with relatively low-tech two-way radios and field manager initiative to keep their delivery fleet peddling and get the job done quickly. An important aspect of effective HR deployment is an understanding of human behavior so that the integration of technology and people capitalizes on the differences rather than creates roadblocks out of them.

Some of the most vivid examples of organizational failures to adequately consider human factors come from recent efforts to implement ERP systems. Westinghouse's implementation of an integrated information system would work only if a fundamental culture change took place. Westinghouse was organized as a highly decentralized group of business units. Enterprise resource planning moved the firm to a centralized, shared environment that would increase organizational efficiency but dramatically alter decision-making independence. Not surprisingly, resistance to the change was formidable and quite effective, as managers argued over trivial details and responded slowly to requests for crucial information. The project was not turned around until Westinghouse realized that all stakeholders, not just direct users, must be convinced of the value and competitive necessity of change. Human resource management should play a pivotal role in managing the integration of people and technology for maximum competitive capability development.

# Creating Small Wins

Karl Weick (1984) introduced a strategy of using "small wins" to create substantial results over time. A small win is a tiny but definite change made in a desired direction. The first step is to modify something relatively easy to transform. This is followed by more easy changes and the multiple small wins eventually add up to both a belief that large-scale change is possible and the experienced reality of a substantial shift in performance. Using a "small wins" strategy can help a firm quickly effectuate large-scale change by identifying individualized time-based goals for employees that lead to the overall desired objectives.

Herb Kelleher of Southwest Airlines is a master of the "small win" strategy. In 1999, studies showed that internal costs were increasing 22% faster than those of other airlines. Kelleher wrote a letter to each employee asking them to save $5 a day. Clearly, $5 a day is a small win when considered in isolation, but when each of those individual $5 savings was aggregated across the firm, the total resulted in a cost savings of 5.6%. Effective resource deployment will often depend on the ability to build upon a series of small wins (Gibson & Blackwell, 1999).

Small wins are more flexible than large-scale change efforts because they enable incremental actions. Small wins are more compatible with fast-paced and unpredictable market changes, because individuals can capitalize on iterative learning and experimentation. Small wins can promote decisive actions that lead to a powerful sense of initiative and momentum, which, over time, can be a source of strategic advantage. A "small wins" strategy allows a firm to select a promising, if not perfect, course of action with an acceptable degree of risk and then act more quickly than rivals.

## Developing Resourceful Employees

Resourcefulness is a combination of creativity and personal initiative that capitalizes on an immediate situation. As rapid deployment specialists, HRM should take a leadership role in developing resourcefulness among individuals and within the firm as a whole. Resourcefulness both encourages quick and effective action and takes advantage of speedy cycle times. Resourcefulness enables people and firms to do more with less and to use all of their resources to full advantage. Keith Hammonds (2001), a Fast Company reporter, tells a story of resourcefulness with impressive competitive consequences. While returning from an interview, he lost his luggage tag in downtown New York City. He did not even realize the tag was missing until he received an unexpected goodies basket from Fisher & Levy catering with his tag attached. Apparently a sales manager had found his tag on the sidewalk and returned it with a note and a generous sample of her firm's brownies, cookies, and other treats. This was such a pleasant surprise that not only did Hammonds write about it (providing free publicity), he planned to use the catering firm for his next event, and shared the goodies and the story with enough other colleagues that a substantial amount of business was generated by one individual act of resourceful kindness.

Teresa Amabile (2000) has identified several specific features of a work environment that can develop resourceful and creative employees. First, creating a sense of challenge by providing opportunities to work on personally important, enriched, and meaningful tasks is necessary. Second, providing employees an opportunity to determine how they carry out their work (autonomy) lays the foundation for resourcefulness. Third, creating a climate of work group support, such as mutual encouragement, constructive feedback on ideas, and shared commitment to the work, facilitates resourcefulness. Fourth, supervisory encouragement that includes providing direction while allowing freedom, providing constructive and positive feedback, and providing mechanisms for open communication and collaboration, stimulates resourcefulness. Fifth, organizational encouragement that emanates from top management supports the development of resourceful capabilities. And sixth, removal of organizational impediments, such as extremely negative criticism of new ideas or an emphasis on maintaining the status quo, clears the way for encouraging resourcefulness. These five factors, in combination, create the environment necessary to encourage individuals to take the risks necessary to develop innovative approaches to workplace problems.

Creating resourcefulness capabilities highlights the changing role of HRM from providing activities and policies to orchestrating processes. At Xerox, for example, a six-step process for problem solving that encourages both individual and organizational learning is used across the organization (Garvin, 1993). Chaparral Steel increases the broad knowledge base of their employees by offering sabbatical programs and training employees in the skills required to perform and evaluate experiments. This develops employees who not only know how things are done (for example, how to control temperature and pressure to align grains of silicon) but also why they occur (for example, understanding the chemical and physical processes that produce the alignment). Processes are needed to encourage employees to try new things and share their successes and failures broadly. Human resource management can orchestrate opportunities for sharing such as internal technology fairs, like those at 3M, and "decision spaces," locations where anyone interested in a topic can meet and contribute (Ghoshal & Bartlett, 1995).

# Do What Is Needed

It is easy to sit in an executive suite and lay out plans for rapidly deploying employees to take advantage of opportunities (or to counter threats) in the marketplace. One may even make plans to move whole divisions of people from one location to another, much like generals moving troops on a battlefield map in a war room. The effectiveness of any plans, however, depends on how well they are implemented. And the effectiveness of implementation depends on the employees themselves.

For rapid deployment of human talent to work well, organizations need employees who can concentrate their efforts when and where needed (flow), sustain performance at high levels (peak performance), and maintain their own well-being while doing so (hardiness). (See Table 6.5.) Earlier, we described how the knowledge economy requires a new right person for the job. Here, we describe how the knowledge economy requires new methods for managing employees for rapid deployment.

Table 6.5 Managing Human Resources for Rapid Deployment

| HR Management Approach | HR Actions |
| --- | --- |
| Cultivate flow. | • Assign individuals to tasks that they find personally important, enriched, and meaningful and that challenge but don't overwhelm them. |
| | • Establish clear goals. |

Nurture peak performance.

- Provide constant feedback.
- Identify projects that are motivating.
- Provide feedback on project progress.
- Provide employees opportunities to work on projects that allow them to learn from and master challenges.
- Encourage employees to build relationships with others.
- Foster a culture in which mistakes are valued as learning experiences rather than "career-enders."

Sustain hardiness.

- Develop hardy attitudes in employees: commitment, control, and challenge.
- Develop hardy coping habits in employees: encourage employees to take a broader perspective of the situation and identify causes that lead to action steps.
- Develop hardy social support in employees: encourage employees to support and assist others as well as seek out encouragement and assistance for themselves.

## Cultivating Flow

Mihalyi Csikszentmihalyi has devoted much of his career as a psychologist to examining what causes people to do things they enjoy but for which they are not rewarded with money, fame, or other recognition. He has studied (among others) chess players, rock climbers, dancers, and composers, who spend countless hours devoted to their activities. What he found in his research is that people do things that they enjoy for sustained periods of time because these activities result in an optimal experience defined as "flow." Flow is a feeling that is expressed by such characteristics as the following.

- **Action and awareness are merged:** Concentration is focused on what we are doing.
- **Distractions are excluded from consciousness:** We are aware of only what is relevant here and now.
- **There is no worry of failure:** Concentration requires too much involvement to consider failure.
- **Self-consciousness disappears:** Concentration leads to minimizing worry about how we appear to other people.
- **The sense of time becomes distorted:** Generally, time is forgotten; experiences that take little time may seem longer, or

experiences that take a long time may seem shorter.

- **The activity becomes autotelic:** Activities are done as ends in themselves, not for a secondary purpose.

Although not all tasks in the workplace can lead to the kind of concentrated engagement described by flow, organizations and managers can take several actions that create and cultivate the environment for flow to emerge. This seems particularly important when employees are asked to align themselves with organizational goals and allow themselves to be rapidly deployed and redeployed as conditions warrant.

Csikszentmihalyi (1990) found that flow experiences were associated with (1) activities that challenge people's skills but don't overwhelm them, (2) activities with clear goals every step of the way, and (3) activities that provide immediate feedback to one's own actions. First, activities that challenge people's skills but don't overwhelm them sustain prolonged effort and concentration. If the challenge is too minimal, boredom results; if the challenge is too great, frustration may occur (either case leads to cessation of effort). Second, clear goals make it so individuals know exactly what to do to accomplish their objectives. For example, the surgeon knows how the incision should proceed moment by moment and the farmer has a plan for planting and harvesting crops. Outcomes are not certain in either case, but individuals feel that they have control over the processes. Third, immediate feedback enables individuals to know exactly how well they are doing. Success or failure can be determined, and corrective action can be implemented when needed. As a rapid deployment specialist, the HRM function can help ensure that individuals who are assembled, concentrated, and deployed are assigned to tasks that challenge but don't overwhelm them, they are given clear goals, and they are provided with constant feedback. This is often important when, for example, employees must work long hours and sustain high levels of effort to meet project deadlines.

## Nurturing Peak Performance

Peak performance is a condition in which individuals exhibit superior performance or productivity. For athletes, the term "personal best" is often used to describe this outcome. Personal peak performance in the workplace was first systematically examined by Charles Garfield (1986). Beginning with studies conducted while he was a computer analyst and leader of engineers, scientists, and support staff on the Apollo 11 project at NASA, Garfield has continued to study high performers in business. What he found in his research was that six conditions led to personal peak performance.

- **Missions that motivate:** Individuals perform at their best when they believe they are doing so for a worthwhile purpose.
- **Results in real time:** Individuals perform at their best when they can see the results of their efforts as they are doing their jobs.
- **Self-management through self-mastery:** Individuals perform at their best when they continuously set their own goals and master challenges.
- **Teambuilding/team playing:** Individuals perform at their best when they can leverage their efforts through collaboration with other people.
- **Course correction:** Individuals perform at their best when they take setbacks as information, mistakes as signals that it is time for a course correction, and when they know how to act decisively as windows of opportunity present themselves.

As a rapid deployment specialist, the HRM function can help ensure that projects have goals that are motivating, individuals are provided feedback on project progress, employees are given opportunities to work on projects that allow them to learn from and master challenges, employees are encouraged to build relationships with others, and a culture is fostered in which mistakes are valued as learning experiences rather than "career-enders."

# Sustaining Hardiness

Salvatore Maddi studied 400 employees at Illinois Bell Telephone before, during, and after the 1970s restructuring of the company that resulted from utility deregulation. He found that while the same external conditions were affecting all employees, about one-third of the employees not only maintained their wellness, they actually thrived during the traumatic experience. On the other hand, two-thirds of the employees suffered both negative physical symptoms and psychological problems as a result of the changes. From his research, Maddi was able to identify attributes of hardiness that distinguished those who maintained their well-being during adversity. Fostering hardiness in employees is especially important when they are being asked to deploy and redeploy; otherwise, employees are likely to experience stress and burnout, resulting in loss of productivity, failure to meet objectives, and potential long-term physical and psychological harm.

Hardiness consists of three components: (1) hardy attitudes, (2) hardy coping, and (3) hardy social support. First, hardy attitudes are powerful attitudes about self, the world, and the interaction between the two that motivate and enable one to engage in performance, leadership, and health enhancing thoughts and behaviors (Maddi, 2000). Hardy attitudes include:

*commitment* to what you are doing, which leads to feelings that it is important and worthwhile enough to engage fully in work tasks, despite stressful change; *control* over yourself to find ways to influence the outcome of stressful changes rather than lapsing into helplessness and passivity; and *challenge*, that is, viewing your situation as a challenge and staying open to the work environment and to the work community, while searching for innovative solutions to problems. Second, hardy coping involves: taking a broader perspective of the stressful situation—reducing its oftentimes overwhelming nature to something more manageable; and understanding the causes of the stressful situation—breaking it down into tangible factors that identify what can be done to resolve it. Third, hardy social support involves giving social support to others in the workplace and getting social support, personal assistance, and encouragement from others. Relationship networks at work, as well as away from work, are powerful moderators of the negative effects of stress. Some organizations offer wellness programs and provide various types of employee assistance plans to their employees to deal with the consequences of stressful work situations. When rapid deployment of human talent is necessary for competitive success in the knowledge economy, more firms will need to provide resources to maintain the well-being of their employees. The role of HRM will be to nurture hardy attitudes, hardy coping skills, and hardy social support among employees. Training programs, such as those offered by the Hardiness Institute (www.hardinessinstitute.com), help develop those capabilities in employees.

# Orchestrating Rapid Deployment

Steve Sell is a high school track coach and one of the best HR rapid deployment specialists we've met. He is able to assemble, train, motivate, and mentally prepare approximately 100 high school student-athletes for each meet. He makes it clear that the team's performance is a function both of individual accomplishments (for example, how fast an individual runs the mile) and of group efforts and coordination (for example, hand-offs among runners on the relay teams). The ten points a runner might earn for winning the 100-yard dash makes little difference if other members of the team do not place in their events. As he says, "your team is only as good as your slowest runner," so teammates consciously push the person in front of them to create overall team success. He values team members who encourage others and bring out their best efforts, since these team members may contribute as much to the team's score as athletes who run faster or jump higher.

Sell models effective training methods, self-discipline, and sportsmanship but stresses that the performance has to come from the team itself. He is incredibly organized and clearly provides the information and instills the sense of responsibility that ensures each athlete is at the right event, with the right equipment, ready to perform at the scheduled time. As the meet progresses, he may need to reassign individuals to different events to respond to injuries or the competition. He instructs distance runners on how take advantage of rivals (for example, draft off the pace-setters). He teaches his runners how to use pacing data and to judge the competitive field accurately. He helps runners develop the mental discipline and confidence to run their own race and the concentration to ignore distracting influences. Small wins (for example, if runners each achieve their own personal best by only a few seconds) can make the difference in the team standing at the track meet.

He never verbally insults or raises his voice to punish an athlete. Instead, he will be completely unresponsive after a disappointing event, to force athletes to personally reflect on their performance and come to terms with how and why they failed to do their best. Yet he is demonstrably proud of any athletes who improve on their personal record even if they are the last runners to cross the finish line. His rules are sparse, clear, and consistently enforced. No one can miss a practice. All distance runners run the last quarter-mile at every workout. New team members must earn their used sweat suits by coming to ten practices, whereas returning lettermen get their new uniforms as soon as they are available.

Many of the things he does to orchestrate his team are designed to promote self-management. He sends the team on runs and puts them on their honor to complete the specified workout, instilling self-discipline and ownership. He talks to the team before meets, asking each student-athlete to set personal goals for each event and leads discussions on how these personal goals can result in team achievements.

He has fostered a sense of team spirit that enables his athletes to run well despite personal adversity (being spiked by an opponent, the ever-present shin splints, and so on) for the good of the team. Sell goes beyond commitment to the team and promotes such a level of pride in the legacy of the school's track program and its commitment to excellence that former student-athletes, like Olympian Jim Ryan, return to periodically inspire (and even run a lap along with) new generations of students. If every HR professional could develop as effective a model for managing human talent as the one Steve Sell has designed for managing his student-athletes, firms would be assured of having the right people, at the right place, at the right time, able to do what needs to be done to ensure organizational success.

# Chapter 7

# New Roles, New Solutions

"In industry, nothing is accomplished except through organization—which means mobilized minds and wills applying energy to carrying out some defined end."

—Tead & Metcalf (1920)

The roles of human capital steward, knowledge facilitator, relationship builder, and rapid deployment specialist capture a very different perspective of HRM from that popularized by Dilbert's "evil HR director," Catbert. Although the caricature portrayed in the cartoon exaggerates the worst of HR practices, it also highlights some of the misplaced focus that has evolved from efforts to provide quite good conventional HRM answers in a world that is asking some entirely different questions. Strategists have reoriented their thinking to go beyond deliberate and long-range planning to incorporate entrepreneurial, emergent, and improvisational approaches that reflect the more unpredictable and fluid competitive landscape of the twenty-first century, HRM needs to rethink its contribution to organizational effectiveness, as well.

Businesses face a new reality and many familiar sources of competitive advantage are eroding (D'Aveni, 1994). Substitutes for natural resources are being invented at a rapid rate, and those natural resources that remain essential are increasingly allocated through political mechanisms or entitlement. National boundaries are less significant than corporate boundaries for defining the scope of business activities. There are fewer protected markets and more market communities. Product technologies provide a fleeting advantage due to short life cycles, leap-frog innovations, discontinuous technology thrusts, and diminishing production cycle times. Many process technologies are widely dispersed across firms and industries. Capital markets are global. Economies of scale have given way to economies of scope. The net result is a competitive playing field that offers fewer and fewer sustained advantages. In the knowledge economy, competitive advantage not only comes from positioning and market power but also from resources and assets, alliances, product and service functionality, customer ties, and an ever increasing array of emerging sources of value creation.

The relentless market shifts have led to the argument that, since a firm's internal characteristics and resources are the fundamental source of value creation, they offer a more reliable and useful foundation for strategic direction setting than an assessment of external conditions (Grant, 1991). This means that a firm's success or failure depends on what resources and capabilities it has (or can create) and on how these resources and capabilities are used. This resource-based view of the firm explains in clear, managerial terms the reasons some firms outperform others.

# Human Resource Management and the Resource-Based View of the Firm

The resource-based view is built on several nested concepts. Robert Grant (1991) provides some of the most useful definitions and distinctions among these concepts. First, **resources** are the basic units of analysis for inputs into the production process. Typical categories of resources include financial resources, physical resources, HR, technological resources, reputational resources, and organizational resources. On their own, most resources offer fairly weak competitive value. Most productive, competitive activity requires collaboration and coordination to orchestrate a bundle of resources, often from different categories. Bundles of resources can yield **strategic capabilities.** Capabilities describe what a firm can do, hopefully more effectively than its rivals. Capabilities are defined as "complex bundles of skills and accumulated knowledge, exercised through organizational processes, that enable firms to coordinate activities and make use of their assets" (Day, 1994: 37). Resources are the fundamental source of a firm's capabilities. Capabilities are the primary source of competitive advantage.

George Stalk, Philip Evans, and Lawrence Shulman (1992) carry this line of reasoning a step further. They argue that to be successful over the long term, most firms must excel at a variety of different kinds of value creation, ranging from insight into changing customer needs, to quick response to technology advances, to innovation and exceptional product design, to efficiency, to prompt response to problems. The need for versatility and excellence, they contend, has changed the logic of strategy from products and positions to a focus on the dynamics of a firm's behaviors (Prahalad & Hamel, 1990; Liedtka, 1999). This means that an essential component of strategy is the processes that orchestrate resources and assets to create capabilities. As a corollary, successful firms make strategic investments in the infrastructure and processes that link together resources and transcend conventional functional partitions. The longer and more complicated the string of activities that transforms a bundle of resources into a capability, the more difficult it is for rivals to duplicate the resulting accomplishments. On the other hand, the more complex the capability, the more challenging it is to achieve or to transfer within the organization that developed it.

The next level of aggregation is **core competence.** C.K. Prahalad and Gary Hamel (1990) define core competence as the "collective learning in an organization" about harmonizing technologies, organizing work, and delivering value. Core competencies are complex bundles of skills, technologies, resources, capabilities, and processes that make a disproportionate contribution to customer value. In this way a core competence promotes competitive uniqueness. Core competencies, they assert, provide the gateway to tomorrow's markets because the outcomes of a core competence have broad application across diverse product and market categories. In addition, core competencies do not wear out or become depreciated over time; rather they are enhanced with use. Persistent application of core competencies widens the gap between the value-creating aptitudes and capacities of the firm having a particular competence and its rivals.

A creative tension is introduced by changeable, and often unpredictable, expectations regarding what is valued for a particular purpose at a particular point in time. Most strategically valuable resources, capabilities, and competencies are path-dependent. This means that they build on prior actions and experience and typically take time to develop. Path-dependency capitalizes on tacit knowledge. Consider, for example, how a master teacher is able to maintain order in a kindergarten classroom without squashing student enthusiasm or creativity. In addition, most strategically valuable resources are socially complex. This means they are realized through people, working in concert, often in a reciprocally interdependent manner that transcends formal job descriptions and reporting relationships. Think, for example, of the improvisational choreography that enables Southwest Airlines employees to maintain their impressive aircraft turnaround times despite variations in people, weather, equipment, luggage, and unexpected problems. Both path-dependency and social complexity tend to reinforce consistent patterns of behavior. The more a particular set of behaviors has been shaped to fit a specific situation, the more difficult it becomes to change the behavioral patterns if the circumstances are radically altered.

The fluid market of the knowledge economy requires superior capabilities and competencies, however, as well as flexibility and versatility. This suggests that strategically useful resources, capabilities, and competencies must be dynamic. Most of a firm's building block resources are inert; they cannot create value without human intervention (Schneier, 1997). In addition, few resources can be bundled into capabilities or orchestrated into competencies without human contributions. Of what use is a high-tech decision support system without a decision maker? Of what value are state-of the-art film, sophisticated cameras, and unique special effects equipment without the artists who create the movie? People not only actualize the value-creating potential resting within other resources, capabilities, and competencies, people offer the primary potential for dynamic action. All of this suggests that a firm's human capital is the trigger and the connective tissue of value creation and reiterates the theme that orchestrating human behavior should be at the center of a firm's strategic initiatives.

# New Human Resource Management Roles for New Human Resource Management Contributions

As we indicated at the beginning, many of the practices and perspectives traditionally found in HRM units are well suited to matching people to jobs, and jobs to strategies, and motivating people to make a variety of different kinds of contributions to value creation expertly and efficiently. Human resource management has become adept at *responding* to the needs of a firm's established strategic intent. We believe that the knowledge economy requires a different contribution from human capital and therefore requires a different kind of HRM. It is time for HRM to take the initiative in designing the basis for competitive value creation. The focus for HR in the knowledge economy should be on making it possible for people to leverage other types of resources, to create capabilities, and to nurture core competencies within a context that rewards both consistency and innovation and values both persistence and flexibility. HRM will provide a greater contribution from maintaining a creative tension than from aligning talented people with established tasks. We suggest that this can best be accomplished if HR professionals embrace four new roles to create fundamental strategic capabilities: human capital steward, knowledge facilitator, relationship builder, and rapid deployment specialist.

As a human capital steward, HRM contributes to strategic capabilities by developing, leveraging, renewing and nurturing a firm's stock of knowledge, skills, abilities, interests, and talents. Human resource management is there to help ensure that every individual is able to make value-added contributions in the knowledge economy by identifying and cultivating individual competencies and capabilities. Moreover, HRM contributes to the firm's strategic capabilities by ensuring that renewal and rejuvenation are ongoing activities rather than episodic events. Resource flexibility, coordination flexibility, and adaptability over time are all important responsibilities of the human capital steward. Although initiatives might include many familiar training and development activities, human capital stewardship also includes creating a culture of continuous learning, inquiry, and personal responsibility for avoiding obsolescence. As human capital steward, HRM shapes the values and provides the contextual backdrop that enables people to take initiative and use their judgment in a flexible and dynamic business setting. The role of HRM is not to create a dependency between the employee and the HR unit but to forge a partnership that leads to increased intellectual capital, enhanced commitment, greater awareness of opportunities to make a difference, and adaptability.

In addition, human capital stewards contribute to strategic capabilities by creating a broad and adjustable pool of human talent. To do this, HRM must design an appropriate mix of core, associate, and peripheral groups of employees, supplemented by flexhire workers, mediated services, contractors, customers, suppliers, and others willing to engage in co-production to improve productivity. An important part of the HR unit's contribution to strategic capabilities comes from transforming potential contributors into actual contributors. If one assumes that a firm rents, rather than owns, intellectual capital, then it becomes apparent that HR professionals will need to devise broad, flexible, customized, and meaningful sets of incentive, reward, and appraisal systems to energize people to want to contribute their best and to look for opportunities to make a difference.

In Gordon MacKenzie's (1992) terminology, human capital stewardship is about helping people achieve orbit.

Orbiting is responsible creativity: vigorously exploring and operating beyond the Hairball of the corporate mindset, beyond *'accepted models, patterns, or standards'*—all the while remaining connected to the spirit of the corporate mission. To find Orbit around a corporate Hairball is to find a place of balance where you benefit from the physical, intellectual and philosophical resources of the organization without becoming entombed in the bureaucracy of the institution.... (p.33) When you come into an organization, you bring with you an arcane potency, which stems, in part, from your uniqueness. That, in turn, is rooted in a complex mosaic of personal history that is original, unfathomable, inimitable. Consequently you can contribute something to an endeavor that nobody else can. There is a power in your uniqueness.... But if you are hypnotized by an organization's culture, you become separated from your personal magic and cannot tap it to help achieve the goals of the organization. In losing connection with your one-of-a-kind magic, you are reduced to nothing more than part of the headcount. It is a delicate balance, resisting the hypnotic spell of an organization's culture and, at the same time, remaining committed from the heart to the personally relevant goals of the organization. But if you can achieve that balance, and maintain it, you will be into orbit (p.53).

Broadly defined, knowledge is at the heart of human capital. Therefore, to be an effective human capital steward, one must also be an expert knowledge facilitator. The two roles are inevitably intertwined. As a knowledge facilitator, an HR professional contributes to developing the root source of organizational capabilities and competencies. What people know, the skills they have honed, the observations that they can interpret, and the situations in which they can act effectively comprise the capabilities and competencies of an organization. There are several themes for HRM to follow in becoming effective knowledge facilitators: expanding the data, intelligence, and information that is available, facilitating access, sorting, and interpretation so that information is useful for action, and maintaining a rich diversity of ideas while seeking agreement on purposes.

As knowledge facilitators, HR professionals must orchestrate a complicated dance that requires both individual mastery and collective artistry. The role of knowledge facilitator is not to teach people what they need to know: often, the technical expertise and specialized information this requires is well beyond the scope of HRM. Rather, knowledge facilitators help individuals learn how to learn. Art Kleiner (1994: 194) defines personal mastery as "the capacity not only to produce results, but also to 'master' the principles underlying the way you produce results. It stems from your ability and willingness to understand and work with the forces around you." As facilitators of individual mastery, HR professionals are personal coaches (to customize a development investment), resource gatherers (to set the stage for learning), "spotters" (for when the learning becomes risky or uncomfortable), and appraisers (to continuously provide feedback regarding the clear competitive value of what is being mastered). Collective knowledge management requires a relationship orientation.

Both effective human capital stewardship and knowledge facilitation depend, in part, on developing a rich network of relationships. The connections among the roles of human capital steward, knowledge facilitator, and that of relationship builder are extensive. The relationship builder role is pivotal since both human capital stewardship and knowledge facilitation work best in the context of an organizational community. Communities are more resilient and more adept at co-evolution with their surroundings than other types of social groupings (Peck, 1987). What does it take to build a community? Communication and relationships in communities go deeper than the typical "masks of composure" found in many workplaces. Communities are noted for their interdependence and mutual respect (Ghoshal & Bartlett, 1995). They are intimate and invite disclosure through ongoing verbal and nonverbal communication (Eisenberg, 1990). Community members share a mutual concern and are committed to resolving problematic conditions faced by others in the web (Weick, 1993). Communities are typically populated by good organizational citizens (Bateman & Organ, 1983). Communities develop an allegiance to the whole enterprise, which, in turn, enables them to balance both individual performance and collective action (Senge, 1990). Communities are the result of complex, genuine, healthy relationships. When HRM creates community relationships across the firm and beyond its borders, it provides a platform for leveraging resources, creating capabilities, and developing core competencies.

Juanita Brown, Bryan Smith, and David Isaacs (1994) offer a number of useful suggestions for the kinds of actions an HR unit might take to help build organizational communities. First, since communities are built around real needs and real work, relationship builders can make valuable contributions by clearly identifying value-added work from historical artifact activities within a firm. Second, simple and robust activities tend to have the greatest and most versatile impact on productivity. Therefore, HR professionals can ferret out and customize those activities that create connections between strategy, values, and behaviors within their own firm-specific environment. Third, communities are built by shared experiences. Therefore, as relationship builders, HR professionals can create experiences in which individuals learn by doing together. Fourth, HRM can build relationships by designing ways to achieve the benefits of co-location without actual proximity. Face-to-face contact must be rich and memorable. Virtual connections need to be constructed to share intimate, revealing, and significant ideas. Finally, Juanita Brown and her colleges suggest that relationship builders find and cultivate what they term "zoysia plugs."

Zoysia is a grass, originally indigenous to Asia, which people sometimes use to start lawns. You water and fertilize plugs of grass scattered far apart. Eventually they find each other and meld into a carpet covering the whole lawn. In organizations, 'zoysia plugs' are people who share your passion. They are also the informal leaders who know how to 'make things happen.' Find them, wherever they might be, and support them however you can. Eventually, when you reach a level of critical mass, you may feel the atmosphere of the entire enterprise shift (Brown et al., 1994: 527).

Therefore, HR professionals can contribute to a firm's ability to leverage its resources and develop strategic capabilities and core competencies by helping individuals build a strong web of relationships. Some of these, such as those within a community of practice, should be quite "sticky" and enduring. Others should be fairly loose and more focused on particular types of transactions or events.

Each of these three roles (human capital steward, knowledge facilitator, and relationship builder) tends to put the greatest emphasis on organizational capacity and readiness. The final HRM role needed in the knowledge economy emphasizes action. As rapid deployment specialists, HR professionals draw on the firm's human capital, knowledge, and relationships to deliver performance quickly, efficiently, flexibly, and with superior effectiveness. For many in HRM, this is a clear departure from the current perspective. Here the focus is on organization-level results. Evaluation of success is not based on whether HRM did its part, but on whether the organization accomplished its strategic intent.

Many firms are experiencing greater competitive aggressiveness as the total number of competitive actions in a field—newly developed market-based moves that challenges the status quo—increase (Ferrier, Smith, & Grimm, 1999). As D'Aveni (1994) argues, persistent strategic success is likely to come from continuous and quite varied competitive activities. Firms that rely on a comparatively simple and narrow range of strategic initiatives increase their vulnerability to performance declines in aggressive and changeable markets (Miller & Chen, 1996). Dynamic competition is driven by the ability to move quickly, take decisive and unexpected action, and thereby confuse and slow the competitive response capabilities of rivals (D'Aveni, 1994). Since the knowledge economy is characterized by aggressive, unprecedented, and quite varied value-creation activities, rapid deployment is a principal source of competitive advantage.

It is important to note, however, that rapid deployment has a reciprocal interdependence with human capital development, relationship formation, and knowledge management. As a firm's cumulative competitive activity increases, new action repertoires, routines, and wisdom about how to carry out competitive moves also expand (Ferrier, Smith, & Grimm, 1999). In this way, these four roles enable HRM to contribute to a firm's strategic capabilities both immediately and into the future. These roles are robust. Drawing from Eccles and Nohria (1992), robust actions are those that accomplish short-term objectives while preserving long-term flexibility.

By adopting these four roles, HRM can become a bridge between a firm's past and its future by capitalizing on path-dependent investments while always searching for new prospects and creative applications of human talent. In combination, these roles enable HRM to embrace both planning and opportunism. Deliberate, decisive actions are coupled with receptiveness to emerging ideas and directions. Organizational learning is juxtaposed with organizational inquiry. Finally, these four new roles encompass a wide variety of activities, perspectives, and challenges. The linking pin is the focus on people as a dominant source of competitive advantage.

# From Human Resources to Strategic Capabilities Unit

So, if the traditional HR function is too constraining to meet the needs of the knowledge economy, how should it be structured to be more responsive? Hubert Saint-Onge provides a blueprint, and Clarica Life Insurance Company in Canada provides a living example of how HR can evolve in the knowledge economy.

Perhaps it's not time for another name change (the change from personnel administration to HRM was traumatic for many), but Saint-Onge labels the new organizational entity a **strategic capabilities unit.** All HRM policies, practices, processes, and programs are integrated with a single, clear focus: linking individual and organizational capability generation to the customer and the overall value-creating strategies of the firm. The organization is structured to enable the reciprocal development of both individual and organizational capability. This is in stark contrast to the traditional HRM function with its silos based on methods and techniques that often lead to an "activity trap" with little impact, and with its controls designed to foster dependent relationships rather than competence creation.

As HR professionals enact these four roles, individuals in organizations are encouraged to embrace self-initiative and collective ownership. They are expected to take full ownership for their own performance, their learning, and their careers. Symbolically, the organization has a "membership contract" with employees rather than an employment contract. The membership contract is based on these guiding principles: "I am my own person," and "My wellbeing depends on the capabilities I acquire through self-initiative." "Members" is also an important concept, because the word "employees" no longer adequately captures the multifaceted relationships that an organization may develop with individuals; anyone who is involved with helping the firm create value for its customers is a "member." Recall in the human capital steward chapter that we discussed numerous sources of human capital that a firm may use, many of which can be found outside its borders.

"Membership Services" replaces the traditional human resource department label, but it, too, has evolved. HR services are provided to employees and managers on three levels. Tier I allows managers and employees to carry out most HR transactions through the intranet and email. Tier 2 provides a live person—or "membership services representative"—(by telephone or in-person) who can resolve issues that cannot be dealt with at Tier 1. Finally, Tier 3 provides an individual capability consultant who can personally intervene to resolve more complex issues when needed.

In addition to membership services, there are "organizational capability consultants" who are members of key business teams throughout the organization. Their purpose is to align leadership, culture, processes, structure, and strategy (that is, facilitate the creation of organizational capability). They play a key role in ensuring that change management processes are complementary with other units throughout the organization. They are also responsible for ensuring the "change readiness" necessary for organizational transformation and renewal.

The "knowledge team" ensures that the technology and people systems are integrated in order to maximally leverage the firm's knowledge assets. They help design the "knowledge depot" (the organization's knowledge repository), as well as facilitate the formation of communities of practice.

Together, the membership services, organizational capability consultants, and knowledge team work to create strategic capabilities for the firm. Success can be measured in enhanced customer relationships, improved agility and coherence in responding to new market trends, accelerated learning, and the acquisition of human and social capital. As

Saint-Onge states, this has transformed Clarica "from a 'make and sell' to a 'sense and respond' organization with the ability to react faster than any competitor to changes in market trends and customer preferences."

Clarica has confronted the challenges of the knowledge economy and transformed its HRM function by removing the old silos of the past. Doing so has enabled them to embrace the new roles of human capital steward, knowledge facilitator, relationship builder, and rapid deployment specialist. Although their particular organizational structure may (or may not) become the blueprint for all HR departments in the knowledge economy, the underlying principles and assumptions on which it is based will certainly prove resilient.

In conclusion, change occurs whether we want it or whether we embrace it. And change *will* come to the HRM function. How change will affect it is uncertain. Continuing to operate along principles and methods that were effective in the industrial era of the twentieth century will only lead to the declining importance of HR professionals and an erosion of their ability to directly contribute to organizational effectiveness. By rethinking the roles of HR in the knowledge economy, however, the HR function may be quite different from what it used to be but will have a large and direct impact on the success of the organization.

# References

## Chapter 1

Berry, L.L. (1995). *On great service: A framework for action.* New York: Free Press.

Fahrenwald, B., Wise, D., & Glynn, D. (2001). *Business Week.*www.businessweek.com/adsections/chain/2.1/chain_index.html.

Huselid, M.A. (1997). Human resource department effectiveness. In L.H. Peters, C.R. Greer, & S.A. Youngblood (Eds.). *The blackwell encyclopedic dictionary of human resource management.* pp.147–148. Malden, MA: Blackwell Publishers.

Intellectualcapital.org: http://intellectualcapital.org/evolution/main.html.6/2/01.

Jacobs, J. (1965). *The death and life of great American cities.* London: Penguin Books.

Jacoby, S.M. (1985). *Employing bureaucracy: Managers, unions, and the transformation of work in American industry 1900–1945.* New York: Columbia University Press.

Kaufman, B.E. (2000). *The theory and practice of strategic HRM and participative management: Antecedents in early industrial relations.* Unpublished manuscript, Georgia State University.

Lengnick-Hall, M.L., & Lengnick-Hall, C.A. (1999). Expanding customer orientation in the HR function. *Human Resource Management Journal. 38* (3), 201–214.

Saint-Onge, H. (2001). What Is Knowledge Management? [On-line] Available: http://www.kno winc.com/saint-onge/library/strategic.htm.5/28/01.

Stewart, T.A. (1997). *Intellectual capital: The new wealth of organizations.* New York: Doubleday.

Stewart, T.A. (July 24, 2000). Water the grass, don't mow, and wait for lightning to strike. *Fortune,* 376–378

Strategic Policy Branch, Industry Canada: htt p://strategis.ic.gc.ca/SSG/pi00009e.html.

Totty, M. (2001). E-Commerce (A Special Report): Overview—The next phase: Contrary to rumor, B-to-B e-commerce is showing surprising signs of life. *The Wall Street Journal* (May 21), R8.

Ulrich, D. (1997). *Human resource champions: The next agenda for adding value and delivering results.* Boston: Harvard Business School Press.

# Chapter 2

Baird, L., & Henderson, J.C. (2001). *The knowledge engine: How to create fast cycles of knowledge-to-performance and performance-to-knowledge.* San Francisco: Berrett-Koehler.

Bartlett, C.A., & Ghoshal, S. (1993). Beyond the M-Form: Toward a managerial theory of the firm. *Strategic Management Journal, 14,* 23–46.

Bohlander, G., Snell, S.A., & Sherman, A. (2001). *Managing human resources.* (12th ed.). Cincinnati, OH: South-Western College Publishing.

Botkin, J. (1999). *Smart business: How knowledge communities can revolutionize your business.* New York: Free Press.

Boyette, J.H., et al., (2001, March). HR in the new economy: Trends and leading practices in human resource management. *PeopleSoft White Paper Series.*

Burton-Jones, A. (1999). *Knowledge capitalism: Business, work, and learning in the new economy.* New York: Oxford University Press.

Cortada, J.W., & Woods, J.A. (Eds.). (1999). *The knowledge management yearbook 1999–2000.* Boston: Butterworth-Heinemann.

Coy, P. (2000). Which companies will thrive in the coming years? Those that value ideas above all else. *Business Week* (August 28), 76–82.

Daft, R.L. (1999). *Leadership: Theory and practice.* Ft. Worth, TX: Dryden Press.

Doz, Y., Santos, J., & Williamson, P. (2001). *From global to metanational: How companies win in the knowledge economy.* Boston: Harvard Business School Press.

Garvin, D.A. (1993). Building a learning organization. *Harvard Business Review, 71* (4), 78–91.

Hamel, G., & Prahalad, C.K. (1993). Strategy as stretch and leverage. *Harvard Business Review, 71* (2), March-April, 75–84.

Hecker, Daniel E. (2001). Occupational employment projections to 2010. *Monthly Labor Review.* Bureau of Labor Statistics: http://www.bls.gov/opub/mlr/2001/11/art4exc.htm.

Huang, K.-T. (1998). Capitalizing on intellectual assets. *IBM Systems Journal, 37* (4). (Reprinted in J.W. Cortada & J.A. Woods (Eds.). *The knowledge management yearbook 1999–2000.* Boston: Butterworth-Heinemann.)

Kaplan, Robert S., & Norton, David P. (2001). *The strategy-focused organization: How balanced scorecard companies can thrive in the new business environment.* Boston: Harvard Business School Press.

Miles, R.E., et al. (1997). Organizing in the knowledge age: Anticipating the cellular form. *Academy of Management Executives, 11* (4), 7–24.

Pascale, R.T. (1999). Surfing the edge of chaos. *Sloan Management Review, 40* (3), 83–94.

Sartain, L. (2001). The future of HR. In *Workplace visions: Exploring the future of work.* (page 7.) Alexandria, VA: Society for Human Resource Management.

Shipper, F., & Manz, C.C. (1992). Employee self-management without formally designated teams: An alternative road to empowerment. *Organizational Dynamics. 20* (3), 48–61.

Tapscott, D. (1996). *The digital economy: Promise and peril in the age of networked intelligence.* New York: McGraw-Hill.

Ulrich, D. (1997). *Human resource champions: The next agenda for adding value and delivering results.* Boston: Harvard Business School Press.

Ulrich, D. (1999). Integrating practice and theory: Towards a more unified view of HR. In P.M. Wright, L.D. Dyer, & J.W. Boudreau (Eds.).

*Strategic human resources management in the twenty-first century* (Supplement 4). New York: Elsevier Science.

# Chapter 3

Barney, J.B. (1995). Looking inside for competitive advantage. *Academy of Management Executives, 9* (4), 49–61.

Becker, G.S. (1964). *Human capital: A theoretical and empirical analysis.* New York: National Bureau of Economic Research.

Block, P. (1993). *Stewardship: Choosing service over self-interest.* San Francisco: Berrett-Koehler.

Bohlander, G., Snell, S.A., & Sherman, A. (2001). *Managing human resources.* (12th ed.). Cincinnati, OH: South-Western College Publishing.

Burton-Jones, A. (1999). *Knowledge capitalism: Business, work, and learning in the new economy.* New York: Oxford University Press.

Coleman, J.S. (1988). Social capital in the creation of human capital. *American Journal of Sociology, 94,* S95–S120.

Cortada, J.W., & Woods, J.A. (Eds.). (1999). *The knowledge management yearbook 1999–2000.* Boston: Butterworth-Heinemann.

Curry, A., & Cavendish, S. (1998). Intellectualcapital.org: http://intellectualcapital.org/evolution/main.html.

Daft, R.L. (1999). *Leadership: Theory and practice.* Ft. Worth, TX: Dryden Press.

Davenport, T.H. (1999). Human capital. *Management Review, 88* (11), 37–42.

Dess, G.G., & Pickens, J.C. (1999). *Beyond productivity: How leading companies achieve superior performance by leveraging their human capital.* New York: American Management Association.

Edvinsson, L., & Malone, M.S. (1997). *Intellectual capital: Realizing your company's true value by finding its hidden roots.* New York: Harper Business.

Hamel, G., & Prahalad, C.K. (1993). Strategy as stretch and leverage. *Harvard Business Review,* March-April, *71* (2), 75–84.

Kaplan, R.S., & Norton, D.P. (2001). *The strategy-focused organization: How balanced scorecard companies thrive in the new business environment.* Boston: Harvard Business School Press.

Kerzner, H. (1989). *Project management: A systems approach to planning, scheduling, and controlling* (3rd ed.). New York: Van Nostrand Reinhold.

Lawler, E.E. (1986). What's wrong with point-factor job evaluation. *Compensation and Benefits Review, 18* (2), 20–28.

Lengnick-Hall, C.A., & Lengnick-Hall, M.L. (1988). Strategic human resources management: A review of the literature and a proposed typology. *Academy of Management Review, 13.*

Lepak, D.P., & Snell, S.A. (1999). The human resource architecture: Toward a theory of human capital allocation and development. *Academy of Management Review, 24* (1), 31–48.

Lev, B. (2002, Jan. 22). Too gray for its own good. *The Wall Street Journal,* p. A12.

Manville, B. (2002). Talking human capital with Professor Gary S. Becker, Nobel Laureate. *Linezine:*http://linezine.com/7.1/interviews/gbbmthc/htm.

Spector, P.E. (1997). KSAOs. In L.H. Peters, C.R. Greer, & S.A. Youngblood (Eds.). *The blackwell encyclopedic dictionary of human resource management.* (p.197.) Malden, MA: Blackwell Publishers.

Stewart, T.A. (1997). *Intellectual capital: The new wealth of organizations.* New York: Doubleday.

Ulrich, D. (1998). Intellectual capital=competence × commitment. *Sloan Management Review,* Winter, 15–26.

Wiener, D.J. (1996). *Burns, falls, and crashes: Interviews with movie stunt performers.* Jefferson, NC: McFarland.

Wright, P.M., & Snell, S.A. (1998). Toward a unifying framework for exploring fit and flexibility in strategic human resource management. *Academy of Management Review, 23* (4), 756–772.

# Chapter 4

Argote, L. (2000). Knowledge transfer: A basis for competitive advantage in firms. *Organizational Behavior and Human Decision Processes, 82* (1), 150–169.

Barth, S. (2000, July 4). Defining knowledge management. *CRM Magazine*.http://www.destinationcrm.com/articles/default.asp?ArticleID=1400.

Buckman, R.H. (1997). Lions and tigers and bears: Following the road from command and control to knowledge sharing. Company white paper, Buckman Laboratories International, Inc.

Burton-Jones, A. (1999). *Knowledge capitalism: Business, work, and learning in the new economy*. New York: Oxford University Press.

Cohen, D. (1997). *Managing knowledge for business success: A conference report*. (Report number 1194-97-CH). New York: The Conference Board, Inc.

Cortada, J.W., & Woods, J.A. (Eds.). (1999). *The knowledge management yearbook 1999-2000*. Boston: Butterworth-Heinemann.

Davenport, T.H. (2000). *Mission critical: Realizing the promise of enterprise systems*. Boston: Harvard Business School Press.

Davenport, T.H., & Prusak, L. (1998). *Working knowledge: How organizations manage what they know*. Boston: Harvard Business School Press.

Davenport, T.H., & Prusak, L. (1999). Working the watercooler. *Across the board*. New York: The Conference Board, Inc.

Doz, Y., Santos, J., & Williamson, P. (2001). *From global to metanational: How companies win in the knowledge economy*. Boston: Harvard Business School Press.

Fell, D. (2001, Sept.). Knowledge management: Bringing the human resources leader to the table. *The next frontier.* Available: www.w orldatwork.org/Content/Infocentral/info-periodical s-frame.html.

Hackett, B. 2000. *Beyond knowledgew management: New ways to work and learn.* New York: The Conference Board, Inc.

Hamel, G., & Prahalad, C.K. (1993). Strategy as stretch and leverage. *Harvard Business Review, 71* (2), 75–84.

Huang, K.-T. (1998). Capitalizing on intellectual assets. *IBM Systems Journal, 37* (4). (Reprinted in J.W. Cortada, & J.A. Woods (Eds.). *The knowledge management yearbook 1999–2000.* Boston: Butterworth-Heinemann.)

Koskiniemi, M. (2001). The human resources role in knowledge management: http://www.worl datwork.org.

Leonard, D., & Sensiper, S. (1998). The role of tacit knowledge in group innovation. *California Management Review, 40* (3): 112–132.

Leonard-Barton, D. (1996). *Wellsprings of knowledge: Building and sustaining the sources of innovation.* Boston: Harvard Business School Press.

Martinez, M.N. (1998, Feb.). The collective power of employee knowledge. *HR Magazine.* (Reprinted in J.W. Cortada, & J.A. Woods (Eds.). *The knowledge management yearbook 1999–2000.* (pp.319–325). Boston: Butterworth-Heinemann.

Neilson, R.E. (2001). Knowledge management: A timeless concept? *The Military Engineer, 93* (611), 35–36.

Prahalad, C.K., & Hamel, G. (1990). The core competence of the corporation. *Harvard Business Review,* May-June, *68* (3), 70–91.

Saint-Onge, H. (1998). *The Antidote,* issue 11. From CSBS: http://www.knowinc.com/saint-onge/articles.htm.

Saint-Onge, H. (2001). Knowledge Management. Available: http://www.knowinc.com/saint-onge/library/strategic.htm.

Salz, P. (2001). Global management for the digital revolution: The 21st century enterprise. *Fortune* (July 23). http://www.fortune.com/sitelets/sections/fortune/corp/2001_07global.html.

Snowden, D. (1998). A method for achieving symbiosis among intellectual assets. (Reprinted in J.W. Cortada & J.A. Woods (Eds.). *The knowledge management yearbook 1999–2000.* (pp.221–232). Boston: Butterworth-Heinemann.)

Stewart, T.A. (1997). *Intellectual capital: The new wealth of organizations.* New York: Doubleday.

Stewart, T.A. (2000, July 24). Water the grass, don't mow, and wait for lightning to strike. *Fortune. 142* (3), 376–377.

Sveiby, K.E. (1998). Tacit knowledge. (Reprinted in J.W. Cortada, & J.A. Woods (Eds.). *The knowledge management yearbook 1999–2000.* (pp.18–27). Boston: Butterworth-Heinemann.)

Ulrich, D., (1998). Intellectual capital=competence × commitment. *Sloan Management Review,* Winter, 15–26.

Ulrich, D. (1998). A new mandate for human resources. *Harvard Business Review, 76* (1), 124–135.

Warren, S. (2002, January 14). I-spy: Getting the lowdown on your competition is just a few clicks away. *The Wall Street Journal*, p. R14.

Webber, A.M. (1993). What's so new about the new economy? *Harvard Business Review, 71* (1), 24–34.

# Chapter 5

Adler, P.S., & Borys, B. (1996). Two types of bureaucracy: Enabling and coercive. *Administrative Science Quarterly, 41* (1), 61–89.

Adler, P.S., & Kwon, S. (2000). Social capital: The good, the bad, and the ugly. In E.L. Lesser (Ed.). *Knowledge and social capital: Foundations and applications.* (pp.89–115). Boston: Butterworth-Heinemann.

Ancona, D., & Caldwell, D. (2000). Compose teams to assure successful boundary activity. In Edwin A. Locke (Ed.). *The blackwell handbook of principles of organizational behavior,* Malden, MA: Blackwell Publishers, Inc.

Brown, J.S., & Duguid, P. (2000). Organizational learning and communities of practice: Toward a unified view of working, learning, and innovation. In E.L. Lesser, M.A. Fontaine, & J.A. Slusher (Eds.). *Knowledge and communities.* (pp.99–122). Boston: Butterworth-Heinemann.

Brown, S.L., & Eisenhardt, K.M. (1998). *Competing on the edge: Strategy as structured chaos.* Boston: Harvard Business School Press.

Capra, F. (1996). *The web of life: A new scientific understanding of living systems.* New York: Anchor Books.

Cohen, D. (1997). *Managing knowledge for business success: A conference report.* (Report number 1194–97–CH). New York: The Conference Board, Inc.

Cohen, D., & Prusak, L. (2001). *In good company: How social capital makes organizations work.* Boston: Harvard Business School Press.

Eisenberg, E.M. (1990). Jamming: Transcendence through organizing. *Communication Research, 17,* 139–164.

Granovetter, M.S. (1973). The strength of weak ties. *American Journal of Sociology, 78,* 1360–1380.

Greenhalgh, L. (2001). *Managing strategic relationships: The key of business success.* New York: Free Press.

Lengnick-Hall, M.L., & Lengnick-Hall, C.A. (1999). Expanding customer orientation in the HR function. *Human Resource Management Journal, 38* (3), 201–214.

Lesser, E., & Prusak, L. (2000). Communities of practice, social capital and organizational knowledge. In E.L. Lesser, M.A. Fontaine, & J.A. Slusher (Eds.). *Knowledge and communities.* (pp.123–132). Boston: Butterworth-Heinemann.

Lussier, R.N., & Achua, C.F. (2001). *Leadership: Theory, application, skill development.* (pp.236–237). South-Western College Publishing.

MacKenzie, G. (1996). *Orbiting the giant hairball: A corporate fool's guide to surviving with grace.* New York: Penguin.

Matson, E., (1997). You can teach this old company new tricks. *Fast Company,* vol. 11 (Oct.-Nov.), 44–46.

Pascale, R.T., Millemann, M., & Gioja, L. (2000). *Surfing the edge of chaos: the laws of nature and the new laws of business.* New York: Random House.

Rivera, P.V. (2001, Sept. 10). 'Boomerang' workers return. *San Antonio Express-News,* p. E1.

Rousseau, D. (1998). Why workers still identify with organizations. *Journal of organizational behavior, 19,* 217–233.

Stewart, T.A. (July 24, 2000). Water the grass, don't mow, and wait for lightning to strike. *Fortune. 142* (3), 367–378.

Uhl-Bien, M., Graen, G.B., & Scandura, T.A. (2000). Implications of leader-member exchange (LMX) for strategic human resource management systems: Relationships as social capital for competitive advantage. In G.R. Ferris (Ed.), *Research in personnel and human resource management: Vol. 18.* (pp.137–185). New York: JAI Press.

Wenger, E. (2000). Communities of practice. In E.L. Lesser, M.A. Fontaine, & J.A. Slusher

(Eds.). *Knowledge and communities.* (pp.3–22). Boston: Butterworth-Heinemann.

# Chapter 6

Amabile, T.M. (2000). Stimulate creativity by fueling passion. In E.A. Locke (Ed.). *Handbook of principles of organizational behavior.* (pp.331–341). Oxford, U.K.: Blackwell Publishers, Ltd.

Barney, J.B. (1995). Looking inside for competitive advantage. *Academy of Management Executives, 9* (4), 49–60.

Borman, W.C., & Motowidlo, S.J. (1993). Expanding the criterion domain to include elements of contextual performance. In Neal Schmitt, Walter C. Borman, and Associates (Eds.). *Personnel Selection in Organizations.* (pp.71–98). San Francisco: Jossey-Bass.

Bowen, D.E. (1986). Managing customers as human resources in service organizations, *Human Resource Management, 25* (3), 371–384.

Bowen, D.E., Ledford, G.E., Jr., & Nathan, B.R. (1991). Hiring for the organization, not the job. *Academy of Management Executives, 5* (4), 35–47.

Campbell, J.P., et al. (1993). A theory of performance. In Neal Schmitt, Walter C. Borman, and Associates (Eds.). *Personnel Selection in Organizations,* (pp.35–70). San Francisco: Jossey-Bass.

Carbonara, P. (1996). "Hire for attitude: Train for skill," *Fast Company, 4,* 73.

Csikszentmihalyi, M. (1990). *Flow: The psychology of optimal experience.* New York: HarperCollins.

Crampton, C.D. (2000, August 6–9). Achieving co-production through interorganizational teams: An intergroup perspective. Presented at the annual Academy of Management meetings in Toronto, Canada.

D'Aveni, R.A. (1994). *Hypercompetition: Managing the dynamics of strategic maneuvering.* New York: Free Press.

Dyer, L. (1984). Linking human resource and business strategies. *Human Resource Planning, 7,* 79–84.

Dyer, L., & Shafer, R.A. (1999). From human resource strategy to organizational effectiveness: Lessons from research on organizational agility. *Research in Personnel and Human Resources Management* (Suppl. 4), 145–174. Stamford, CT: Jai Press.

Eisenhardt, K.M., & Tabrizi, B.N. (1995). Accelerating adapative process: Product innovation in the global computer industry. *Administrative Science Quarterly, 40* (1), 84–111.

Fine, C.H. (1998). *Clockspeed: Winning industry control in the age of temporary advantage.* Reading, MA: Perseus Books.

Garfield, C.A. (1986). *Peak performers: The new heroes of American business.* New York: William Morrow & Company.

Garvin, D. (1993). Building a learning organization. *Harvard Business Review, 71* (4), 78–91.

Ghoshal, S., & Bartlett, C.A. (1995). Changing the role of top management: Beyond structure to processes. *Harvard Business Review, 73* (1), 86–96.

Gibson, J.W., & Blackwell, C.W. (1999). Flying high with Herb Kelleher: A profile in charismatic leadership. *The Journal of Leadership Studies, 6,* 120–137.

Hamel, G., & Prahalad, C.K. (1993). Strategy as stretch and leverage. *Harvard Business Review, 71* (2), 75–85.

Hammonds, K.H. (2001). A heartbreaking gesture of staggering kindness. *Fast Company.* (March) http://www.fastcompany.com/lead/lead_fe ature/good_service.html.

Kaplan, R.S., & Norton, D.P. (2001). *The strategy-focused organization: How balanced scorecard companies can thrive in the new business environment.* Boston: Harvard Business School Press.

Lengnick-Hall, C.A. (1996). Customer contributions to quality: A different view of the customer-oriented firm. *Academy of Management Review, 21* (3), 791–824.

Lengnick-Hall, C.A., & Lengnick-Hall, M.L. (1988). Strategic human resources management: A review of the literature and a proposed typology. *Academy of Management Review, 13,* 454–470.

Lengnick-Hall, M.L., & Lengnick-Hall, C.A. (1999). Expanding customer orientation in the HR function. *Human Resource Management Journal, 38* (3), 201–214.

MacDuffie, J. (1995). Human resource bundles and manufacturing performance: Organizational logic and flexible-production systems in the world auto industry. *Industrial and Labor Relations Review, 48,* 197–221.

Manz, C.C., & Sims, H.P. Jr. (1980). Self-management as a substitute for leadership: A social learning perspective. *Academy of Management Review, 5,* 361–367.

Matson, E. (1996). Speed kills (the competition). *Fast Company, 4:* 84.

Mills, P.K., Chase, R.B., & Margulies, N. (1983). Motivating the client/employee system as a service production strategy. *Academy of Management Review, 8,* 301–310.

Pfeffer, J., & Veiga, J.F. (1999). Putting people first for organizational success. *The Academy of Management Executives, 13,* 37–48.

Pulakos, E.D., et al. (2000). Adaptability in the workplace: Development of a taxonomy of adaptive performance. *Journal of Applied Psychology, 85,* 612–624.

Salter, C. (2000). Built to scale. *Fast Company, 36:* 348–353.

Schneider, B. & Bowen, D.E. (1995). *Winning the service game.* Boston: Harvard Business School Press.

Shafer, R.A., et al. (2001). Creating a human resource strategy to foster organizational agility: A case study. *Human Resource Management, 40* (3), 197–211.

Simons, Anna. J. (1997). *The company they keep: Life inside the U.S. Army special forces.* New York: Avon Books.

Snow, C.C., & Snell, S.A. (1993). Staffing as strategy. In N. Schmitt, W.C. Borman, & Associates (Eds.). *Personnel selection in organizations.* (pp.448–478). San Francisco: Jossey-Bass Publishers.

Tapscott, D. (1995). *The digital economy: Promise and peril in the age of networked intelligence.* New York: McGraw-Hill.

United States Marine Corps (1989). *Warfighting: The U.S. Marine Corps book of strategy.* New York: Currency Doubleday.

Volberta, H.W. (1996). Toward the flexible form: How to remain vital in hypercompetitive environments. *Organization Science, 7* (4), 359–373.

Vroom, V.H., & Jago, A. (1988). *The new leadership: Managing participation in organizations.* Englewood Cliffs, NJ: Prentice-Hall.

Weick, K. (1984). Small wins. *American Psychologist, 39,* 40–49.

Wright, P.M., & Snell, S.A. (1998). Toward a unifying framework for exploring fit and flexibility in strategic human resource management. *Academy of Management Review, 23* (4): 756–772.

# Chapter 7

Bateman, T.S., & Organ, D.W. (1983). Job satisfaction and the good soldier: The relationship between affect and employee "citizenship." *Academy of Management Journal, 26,* 587–595.

Brown, J., Smith, B., & Isaacs, D. (1994). Operating principles for building community. In P.M. Senge, C. Roberts, R.B. Ross, B.J. Smith, & A. Kleiner (Eds.). *The fifth discipline fieldbook: Strategies and tools for building a learning organization.* New York: Currency-Doubleday.

D'Aveni, Richard A. (1994). *Hypercompetition: Managing the dynamics of strategic maneuvering.* New York: Free Press.

Day, G. (1994). The capabilities of market-driven organizations. *Journal of Marketing, 58,* 37–52.

Eccles, R.G., & Norhia, N. (1992). *Beyond the hype: Rediscovering the essence of management.* Boston: Harvard Business School Press.

Eisenberg, E.M. (1990). Jamming: Transcendence through organizing. *Communication Research, 17,* 139–164.

Ferrier, W.J., Smith, K.G., & Grimm, C.M. (1999). The role of competitive action in market share erosion and industry dethronement: A study of industry leaders and challengers. *Academy of Management Journal, 42* (4), 372–388.

Ghoshal, S., & Bartlett, C.A. (1995). Changing the role of top management: Beyond structure to process. *Harvard Business Review, 73* (1), 86–96.

Grant, R.M. (1991). The resource-based theory of competitive advantage. *California Management Review, 33,* 3.

Kleiner, A. (1994). Mastery. In P.M. Senge, C. Roberts, R.B. Ross, B.J. Smith, & A. Kleiner (Eds.). *The fifth discipline fieldbook: Strategies and tools for building a learning organization.* New York: Doubleday.

Liedtka, J. (1999). Linking competitive advantage with communities of practice. *Journal of Management Inquiry, 8* (1), 5–16.

MacKenzie, G. (1992). *Orbiting the giant hairball: A corporate fool's guide to surviving with grace.* New York: Penguin Putnam Inc.

Miller, D., & Chen, M. (1996). The simplicity of competitive repertoires: An empirical analysis. *Strategic Management Journal, 17,* 419–440.

Peck, M.S. (1987). *The different drum.* New York: Simon & Schuster.

Schneier, R. (1997). People value added the new performance measure. *Strategy and Leadership, 25* (2), 14–18.

Senge, P.M. (1990). *The fifth discipline: The art and practice of the learning organization.* New York: Doubleday.

Stalk, G., Evans, P., & Shulman, L.E. (1992). Competing on capabilities: the new rules of corporate strategy. *Harvard Business Review, 70* (3), 57–69.

Prahalad, C.K., & Hamel, G. (1990). The core competence of the corporation. *Harvard Business Review, 68* (3), 70–91.

Weick, K. (1993). The collapse of sensemaking in organizations: The Mann Gulch disaster. *Administrative Science Quarterly, 38,* 628–652.

# About the Authors

*Mark L. Lengnick-Hall,* Ph.D., is a Professor of Management in the College of Business at the University of Texas at San Antonio. He has human resource management experience in both private industry and state government. Dr. Lengnick-Hall has also consulted with and provided training for numerous organizations.

His articles have been published in journals such as the *Academy of Management Review, Human Resource Management Review, Human Resource Management, Personnel Psychology, Personnel, Journal of Organizational Behavior, Organization Development Journal, HR Magazine, Training and Development, Employee Responsibilities and Rights Journal, Health Progress, Public Personnel Management,* and the *Journal of Management Education.* He has co-authored two books: *Compensation Decision Making: A Computer-Based Approach,* published by Dryden in 1994, and *Interactive Human Resource Management and Strategic Planning,* published by Quorum in 1990. Dr. Lengnick-Hall has also contributed chapters to other books.

His current research interests include strategic human resource management, employment issues pertaining to disabled workers, and implementing information technology in organizations.

***Cynthia A. Lengnick-Hall,*** Ph.D., is a Professor of Management in the College of Business at the University of Texas at San Antonio. She has consulting and management experience in both private industry and higher education administration. Dr. Lengnick-Hall has consulted with and provided executive education for a number of organizations.

Her articles have been published in journals such as the *Academy of Management Review, Academy of Management Journal, Strategic Management Journal, Journal of Management, Journal of Engineering and Management Technology, Human Resource Management, Strategy and Leadership, Organization Development Journal, Organization Studies, Journal of Organizational Behavior, Employee Responsibilities and Rights Journal, Health Progress, Hospital and Health Service Administration,* and the *Journal of Management Education.* She has co-authored two books: *Experiencing Quality,* published by Dryden in 1995, and *Interactive Human Resource Management and Strategic Planning,* published by Quorum in 1990. Dr. Lengnick-Hall has also contributed chapters to several other books.

Her current research interests include strategic analysis, achieving competitive superiority in high-velocity environments, designing complex adaptive organizations, using information technology as a platform for social capital development, and strategic human resource management.